ORNAMENTAL DESIGN

ORNAMENTALE KUNST
MOTIFS ORNEMENTAUX
DESIGN ORNAMENTALE
EL DISEÑO ORNAMENTAL

1850

ORNAMENTAL DESIGN

ORNAMENTALE KUNST
MOTIFS ORNEMENTAUX
DESIGN ORNAMENTALE
EL DISEÑO ORNAMENTAL

1850

THE PEPIN PRESS

Copyright for this edition
© 1996, 1998 The Pepin Press B/v

First published in 1996 by The Pepin Press
Reprinted in 1998

Copyright introduction 'Ornamental Design 1850'
© 1996, 1998 Pepin Van Roojen

ISBN 90 5496 030 2

The Pepin Press
POB 10349 • 1001 EH Amsterdam • The Netherlands
Tel (+) 31 20 4202021 • Fax (+) 31 20 4201152 • e-mail:pepin@euronet.nl
Printed in Singapore

Ornamental Design 1850

The material presented in this book was originally published in the early 1870s, and representative of styles prevalent in the preceding decades. This was a period during which ornamental design became increasingly widespread, but, ironically, not a time during which many new designs were developed. Instead, the past was raided by architects, artists and craftsmen, and shapes and patterns that at one point in history may have had revered meanings, were copied, altered, combined or split to pieces, without much consideration for their original purpose. However, the result is a wealth of beautiful design. Practically every ornamental style known to early and mid-nineteenth century Europeans, from ancient Egyptian to Baroque, is represented here. The main items illustrated are ceramics, metalware, glass objects, furniture, carpets and other textiles, either complete, or in detail. There are also some architectural elements and examples of interior decoration.

Design inspired by ancient ancient Egypt displays the presence of stylised lotus flowers, motifs reminiscent of hieroglyphs, zig-zag patterns and spiralling constructions. Many examples of Greek ornamental design were copied from friezes on which mythical events were recorded. Very popular Greek ornaments are fret, spiral and bead borders, variations on the echinus (egg and dart), the acanthus and rosettes and palmettes. A principal characteristic of Greek design is the use of columns in architecture and interiors, topped with elaborate capitals. Very simply put, Roman adornment seems to have been largely an exuberant extension of the Greek visual vocabulary, with Etruscan elements added. Some of the mosaic designs in this book were clearly based on Pompeian originals. The so-called Byzantine school is a blending of styles: Greek, Roman, and early Christian ornaments, combined with elements from Persia and Syria. Byzantine ornamentation was one of the sources of Islamic decorative style, with elaborate geometrical patterns due to the interdiction of representations of living things. Illustrative of the Moorish style are the inter-woven formations based on Arabic calligraphy. The Gothic period contributed, among others, variations on the clover leaf: trefoils, quatrefoils and cinquefoils, but also the fleur-de-lis and the Tudor rose. During the Renaissance, the classical Greco-Roman models were rejuvenated and complemented with elements from the Near Orient. Especially in architecture, classical orders were followed. In ornamental design, freer patterns became fashionable. Of course, the Renaissance motifs used during the period covered by this book, were, again, often combined with other styles.

As with other volumes in The Pepin Press Design Book series, the intention of this book is not to provide a complete survey of ornamental design, but to offer high quality reproductions of outstanding examples, as sources of reference and inspiration for designers and architects.

Ornamentale Kunst um 1850

Das in diesem Band zusammengetragene Material wurde erstmals in den frühen siebziger Jahren des 19. Jahrhunderts veröffentlicht. Es ist ein Zeugnis der Stilformen, die in den vorangegangenen fünfzig Jahren die ornamentale Kunst beherrschten, eine Epoche, in der die dekorative Formgebung zwar eine immer wichtigere Rolle spielte, ironischerweise jedoch kaum selbst neue Formen entwickelte. Im Gegenteil, Architektur, Kunst und Kunstgewerbe nahmen sich nach Belieben historische Stilrichtungen zum Vorbild. Formen und Motive, die einmal einen Darstellungsinhalt hatten, wurden ohne Rücksicht auf deren ursprüngliche Bedeutung kopiert, abgewandelt, zusammengefügt oder auszugsweise übernommen. Wie dem auch sei, das Ergebnis ist unbestrittenermaßen eine Fülle wunderschöner Formen. Fast jede ornamentale Stilrichtung, die im Europa des Anfangs und der Mitte des 19. Jahrhunderts bekannt war – von Formen des alten Ägypten bis hin zum Barock –, ist in diesem Band zu finden. In der vorliegenden Ausgabe sind sowohl ganze Gegenstände als auch Details abgebildet. In erster Linie handelt es sich dabei um Keramiken, Metallarbeiten, Glas, Teppiche und sonstige Gewebe sowie Möbel. Darüber hinaus sind einige Beispiele aus der Baukunst und der Innenarchitektur vertreten.

Formen, die sich an altägyptische Vorbilder anlehnen, zeigen sich in stilisierten Lotusblüten, in Motiven, die an Hieroglyphen erinnern, in Zickzack- und Spirallinien. Viele Beispiele griechischer Ornamentik wurden von Friesen mit Darstellungen mythologischer Ereignisse kopiert. Besonders beliebt waren in diesem Zusammenhang Zier-, Spiral- und Perlleisten, Variationen auf das Eierstabmuster, das Akanthusblatt sowie Rosetten und Palmetten. Ein grundlegendes Merkmal griechischer Kunst ist die Verwendung von Säulen mit plastisch ausgearbeiteten Kapitellen in Baukunst und Innenarchitektur. Römische Formelemente kann man im großen und ganzen als eine reichgeschmückte Weiterentwicklung des griechischen optischen Inventars mit Hinzufügung etruskischer Elemente bezeichnen. Einige der in diesem Band abgebildeten Mosaiken haben eindeutig pompejische Vorbilder. Die sogenannte Byzantinische Schule ist eine Mischung vieler Stilrichtungen: griechische, römische und altchristliche Ornamentik mit persischen und syrischen Elementen. Die byzantinische Ornamentik war eine der Quellen für den islamischen Dekorativstil, der sich vor allem aufgrund des Verbots der Darstellung alles Lebendigen in die Richtung nuancierter, geometrischer Muster weiterentwickelt hat. Für die maurische Kunst sind sich an die arabische Kalligraphie anlehnende, miteinander verflochtene Formen kenn-zeichnend. Anleihen aus der Gotik sind unter anderem in Form von Kleeblatt-variationen in drei-, vier- und fünfblättrigen Darstellungen sowie der Französischen Lilie und der Tudorrose zu finden. In der Renaissance wurden die klassischen römischen Vorbilder wieder zum Leben erweckt und um Elemente aus dem Nahen Osten ergänzt. Vor allem in der Baukunst wurden klassische Ordnungen befolgt. In die ornamentale Kunst hielten freiere Formen Einzug. Auch die in diesem Band vertretenen Renaissancemotive wurden oft mit anderen Stilrichtungen kombiniert.

Wie auch bei anderen Ausgaben der Pepin Press Design Book-Serie ist es nicht Ziel, einen vollständigen Überblick zu verschaffen, sondern vielmehr zeitgenössischen Designern und Architekten herausragende Vorbilder als Inspirationsquelle und als Referenzmaterial in erstklassiger Reproduktionsqualität anzubieten.

Motifs Ornementaux 1850

Les motifs présentés dans ce livre furent publiés pour la première fois au début des années 1870 et sont représentatifs de styles qui étaient répandus un demi siècle plus tôt environ. Au cours de cette période, les motifs ornementaux devinrent de plus en plus fréquents mais ironiquement, peu de nouveaux motifs furent élaborés. En fait, le passé fut pillé en masse par les architectes, les artistes et les artisans et des formes et motifs qui à un certain moment de l'histoire avaient pu avoir une signification vénérée furent copiés, modifiés, combinés ou scindés en nombreux éléments, sans beaucoup d'égards pour leur signification originale. Quoi qu'il en soit ils nous ont fourni de ce fait une multitude de motifs magnifiques. Pratiquement tous les styles ornementaux connus des européens du début et du milieu du dix-neuvième siècle, de l'Egypte ancienne au Baroque, sont représentés ici. Les illustrations présentées dans ce livre concernent des objets complets ou des détails d'objets. Les principaux articles illustrés sont des objets en céramique, en métal et en verre, des tapis et autres textiles et des meubles. Il y a également quelques éléments architecturaux et exemples de décoration intérieure.

Les motifs inspirés de l'Egypte ancienne révèlent la présence de fleurs de lotus stylisées, de motifs s'inspirant de hiéroglyphes, de motifs en zigzag et de constructions en spirales. De nombreux exemples de motifs ornementaux grecs se sont inspirés de frises sur lesquelles des événements mythiques étaient relatés. Parmi les décorations grecques très prisées on trouve les bordures chantournées, en spirales et à perles, des variations sur l'echinus (oeuf et flèche), l'acanthus ainsi que des rosaces et des palmettes. L'une des principales caractéristiques du style grec est la présence de colonnes en architecture et dans les intérieurs, surmontées de chapiteaux élaborés. Pour simplifier, le style décoratif romain semble avoir été dans une vaste mesure, une prolongation exubérante du vocabulaire visuel grec avec en plus, quelques éléments étrusques. Certains motifs de mosaïques présentés dans ce livre se sont de toute évidence inspirés d'originaux pompéiens. Ce que l'on appelle l'école byzantine constitue en elle-même un mélange de styles: des éléments décoratifs grecs, romains et du début de l'ère chrétienne auxquels viennent s'ajouter des éléments venus de Perse et de Syrie. Les motifs byzantins furent l'une des sources d'inspiration du style décoratif islamique, mais ce dernier s'orienta ensuite davantage vers des motifs géographiques élaborés. Cela s'explique bien sûr par l'interdiction de représenter des créatures vivantes. Les motifs entrelacés basés sur la calligraphie arabe illustrent le style maure. La période gothique apporta entre autres des variations sur la feuille de trèfle: trèfle à trois feuilles, à quatre feuilles et à cinq feuilles mais également les fleurs de lis et la rose Tudor. Au cours de la Renaissance, les modèles classiques gréco-romains furent rajeunis et complétés avec des éléments empruntés au Proche-Orient. L'architecture en particulier continua à obéir aux règles classiques. Par contre, au niveau des motifs ornementaux, des styles plus souples devinrent à la mode. Bien entendu, les motifs de la Renaissance utilisés pendant la période couverte par ce livre étaient, là encore, souvent alliés à d'autres styles.

Comme d'autres volumes de la série The Pepin Press Design Book, ce livre ne cherche pas à fournir un panorama complet mais à offrir des reproductions de qualité d'exemples de styles remarquables afin de fournir une source de référence et d'inspiration aux concepteurs et architectes d'aujourd'hui.

Design Ornamentale 1850

Il materiale presentato in questo libro venne originariamente pubblicato poco dopo il 1870, e offre un esempio degli stili prevalenti nel mezzo secolo precedente. Questo fu il periodo in cui il design ornamentale acquistò sempre maggiore importanza, ma non, paradossalmente, un'epoca in cui vennero sviluppate molte nuove forme. Invece architetti, artisti e artigiani saccheggiarono il passato, e forme e figure che in un certo periodo storico potevano anche essere oggetto di venerazione, vennero copiate, alterate, combinate o fatte a pezzi, senza molta considerazione per il loro proposito originale. Il risultato è che ora abbiamo a disposizione un'abbondanza di magnifico design. Viene qui rappresentato praticamente ogni stile ornamentale noto agli Europei della prima metà dell'Ottocento, dall'antico Egitto al Barocco. Le illustrazioni in questo libro possono essere oggetti completi o dettagli: ceramiche, oggetti di metallo, vetri, tappeti e altri tessuti, mobili. Il libro presenta inoltre alcuni elementi architettonici ed esempi di arredamento.

Il design che s'ispira all'antico Egitto presenta fiori di loto stilizzati, motivi che ricordano geroglifici, disegni a zig-zag e costruzioni a spirale. Molti esempi di decorazione ornamentale greca vennero copiati da fregi su cui erano stati immortalati eventi mitici. Ornamenti greci molto popolari sono margini a greca, a spirale e a perle, variazioni sull'echino (uovo e freccia), l'acanto, le rosette e le foglie di palma. Una caratteristica principale dell'ornamentazione greca è l'uso delle colonne in architettura e negli interni, con in cima elaborati capitelli. In parole povere, l'ornamento romano sembra essere stato in larga misura un'esuberante estensione del vocabolario visivo greco, con l'aggiunta di elementi etruschi. Alcuni dei disegni di mosaici presenti in questo libro si basano chiaramente su originali pompeiani. La cosidetta scuola bizantina rappresenta anch'essa la fusione di numerosi stili: ornamentazione greca, romana, paleo-cristiana, con elementi tratti dalla Persia e dalla Siria. L'ornamentazione bizantina fu una delle fonti dello stile decorativo islamico, anche se quest'ultimo si orientò verso elaborati disegni geometrici, un effetto naturalmente della proibizione di rappresentare cose viventi. Esempi dello stile moresco sono i tessuti che si basano sulla grafia araba. Il periodo gotico creò, tra l'altro, le variazioni sul trifoglio, a tre, a quattro a cinque foglie, ma anche il fiordaliso, e la rosa dei Tudor. Durante il Rinascimento, i modelli classici greco-romani vennero recuperati e uniti a elementi provenienti dal vicino Oriente. Specialmente nel campo dell'architettura, venivano seguiti gli ordini classici. Nella decorazione ornamentale divennero di moda delle forme più libere. Naturalmente i motivi rinascimentali usati nel periodo illustrato nel libro, erano, ancora una volta, spesso combinati ad altri stili.

Come con altri volumi della serie The Pepin Press Design Book, l'intenzione di questo libro non è quella di offrire un visione generale completa, ma una riproduzione di alta qualità di straordinari esempi di design, come fonte di riferimento e ispirazione per i designer e gli architetti di oggi.

El Diseño Ornamental 1850

El material que se presenta en este libro fue publicado originalmente en los principios de los 1870, y representaba los estilos que prevalecían durante el medio siglo anterior. Fue durante este período que el diseño ornamental comenzaba cada vez más a prevalecer, pero, irónicamente, no fue una época en la que muchos nuevos diseños fueron desarrollados. En cambio, los arquitectos, los artistas y los artesanos hicieron grandes irrupciones del pasado, y las formas y patrones que en un momento de la historia podían haber tenido una significación venerada, fueron copiados, cambiados, combinados o divididos en pedazos, sin considerar su propósito original. Sin embargo, el resultado es que ello nos ha dotado de una riqueza de diseños bellos. Prácticamente todos los estilos ornamentales conocidos por los europeos de la primera parte del siglo diecinueve, desde los egipcios antiguos hasta el barroco, están representados aquí. Las ilustraciones que se encuentran en este libro pueden considerarse como objetos completos o como detalles. Las principales ilustraciones son de artefactos de cerámica y de metal, de objetos de vidrio, de alfombras y otros textiles y de muebles. También hay algunos elementos arquitectónicos y ejemplos de decoración interior.

Los diseños inspirados por el Egipto Antiguo demuestran la presencia de las flores estilizadas del loto, motivos recordativos de jeroglíficos, patrones en zigzag y construcciones espirales. Muchos ejemplos del diseño ornamental griego fueron copiados de los frisos representando eventos míticos. Ornamentos griegos muy populares son bordes de calados, espirales y pestañas, variaciones del equino (huevo y dardo), el acanto, y rosetónes y palmas. Una característica importante del diseño griego es el uso de columnas en la arquitectura y los interiores, coronadas de capiteles elaborados. Muy sencillamente expuesto, el adorno romano parece ser en la mayoría una extensión exuberante del vocabulario visual griego, con elementos etruscos agregados. Algunos de los diseños de mosaicos en este libro están claramente basados en originales pompeyanos. La llamada escuela bizantina es en si misma una mezcla de estilos: ornamentación griega, romana y de los primeros cristianos, junto con elementos desde Persia y Siria. La ornamentación bizantina fue una de las fuentes del estilo decorativo islámico, pero esto se cambió hasta incorporar patrones elaborados geométricos. Esto se debía, por supuesto, a la prohibición de representar seres vivos. Las formaciones entrelazadas basadas en la caligrafía árabe son una ilustración del estilo morisco. Entre otros aspectos, la época gótica introdujo variaciones de la hoja del trébol; trifolio, cuatrifolio y quinquefolio, además de la flor de lis y la rosa Tudor. Durante el Renacimiento, los modelos clásicos griego-romanos fueron rejuvenecidos y complementados con elementos del Levante. Especialmente en la arquitectura, se seguían ordenes clásicos. En el diseño ornamental, los patrones libres llegaron a estar de moda. Por supuesto, los motivos del Renacimiento que se usaban durante el período cubierto en este libro eran, otra vez, frecuentemente combinados con otros estilos.

Así como en otros volúmenes en la serie del Pepin Press Design Books, el propósito de este libro es el de proveer no una revisión completa, sino una reproducción de categoría, basada en ejemplos destacados de diseño, como una fuente de referencia y una inspiración para los diseñadores y arquitectos de hoy en día.

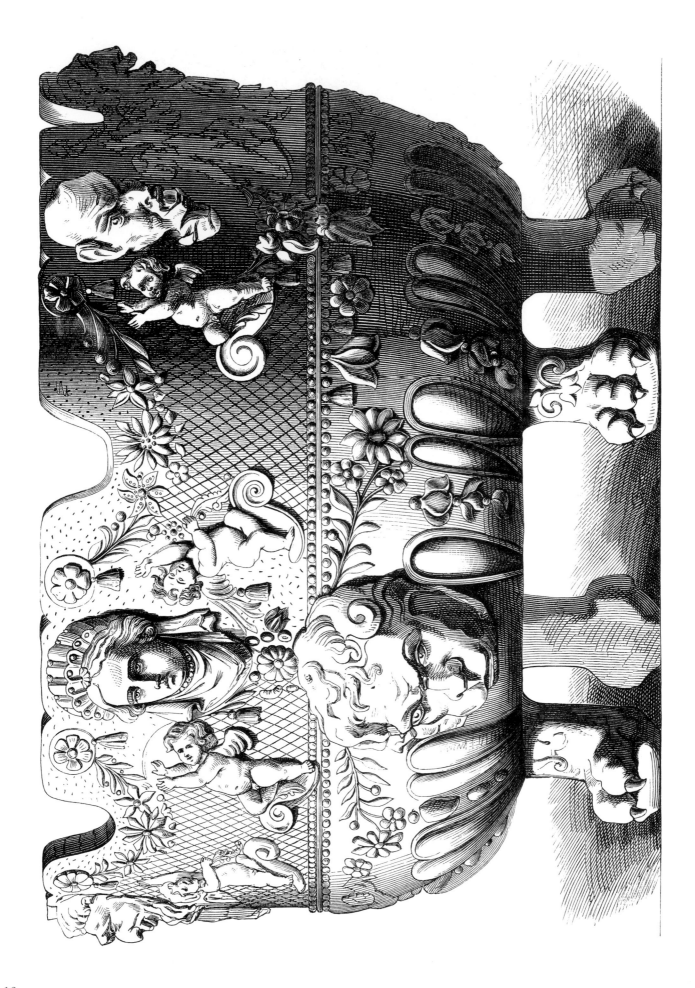

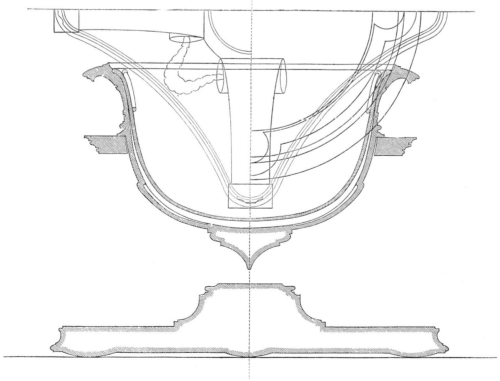

13

14

24

29

31

33

40

43

44

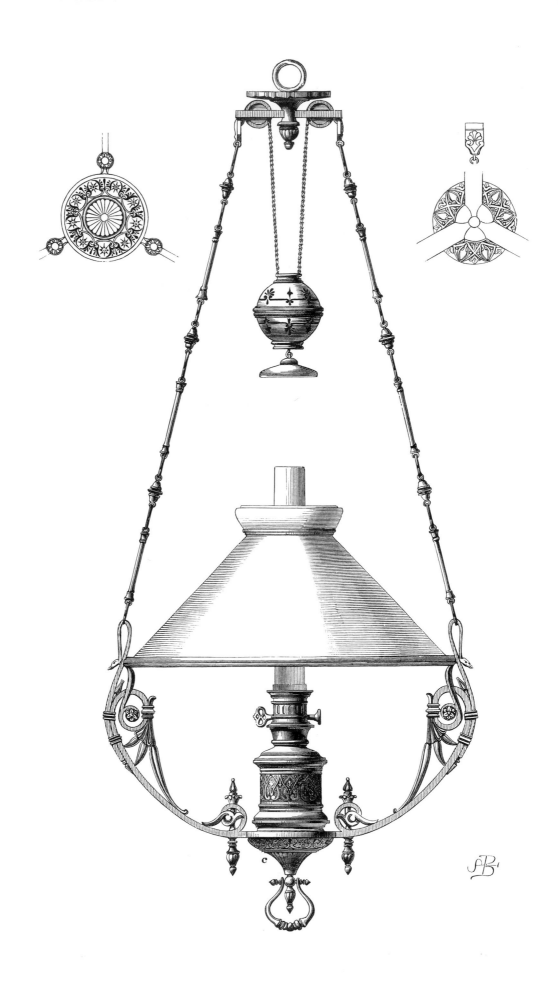

46

CRNANTIBUS ALMA

48

49

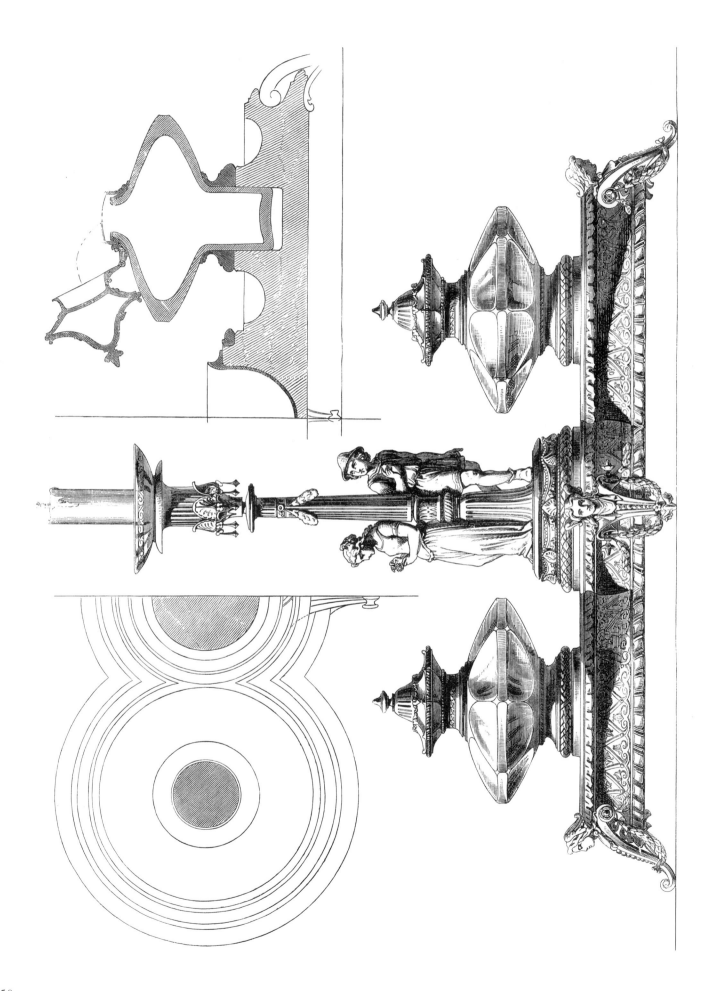

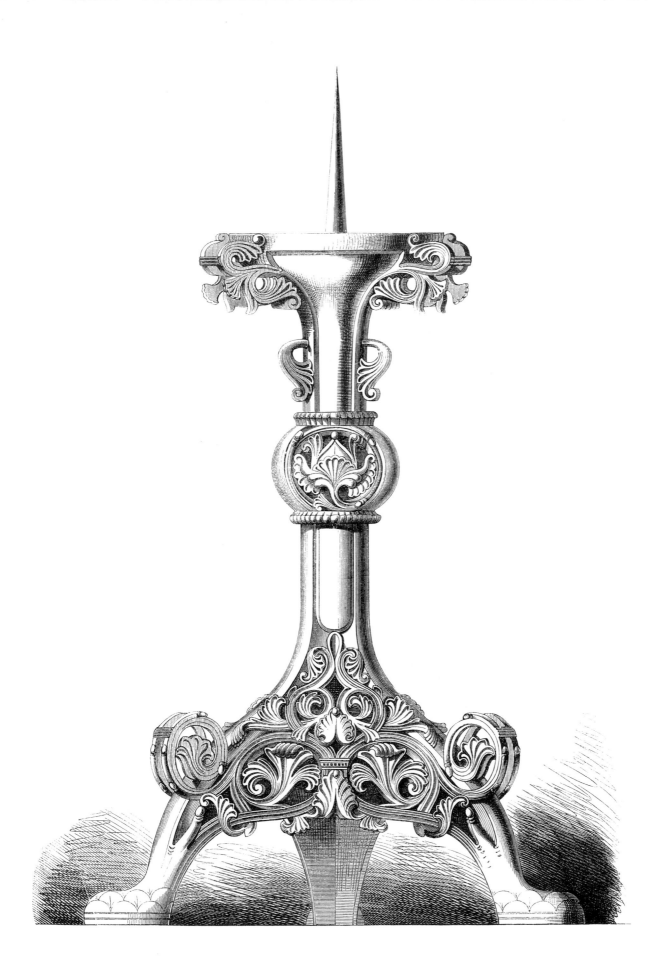

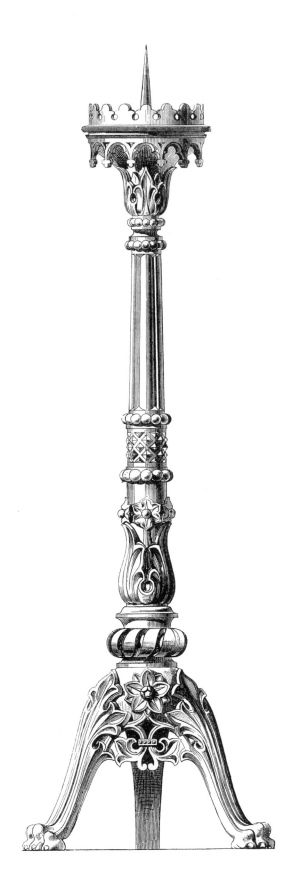

54

55

62

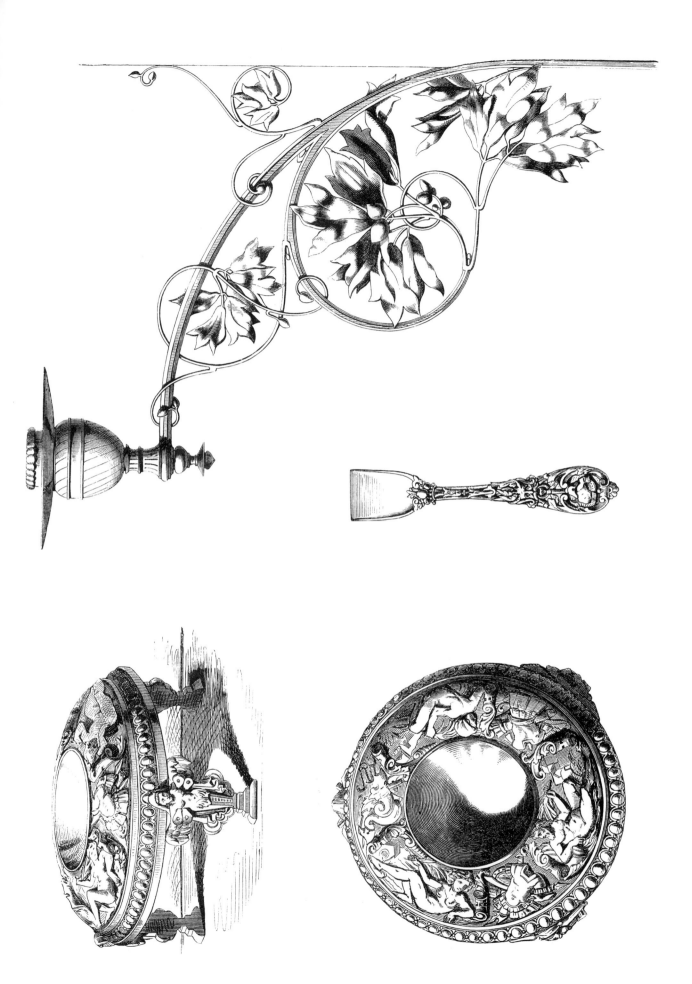

70

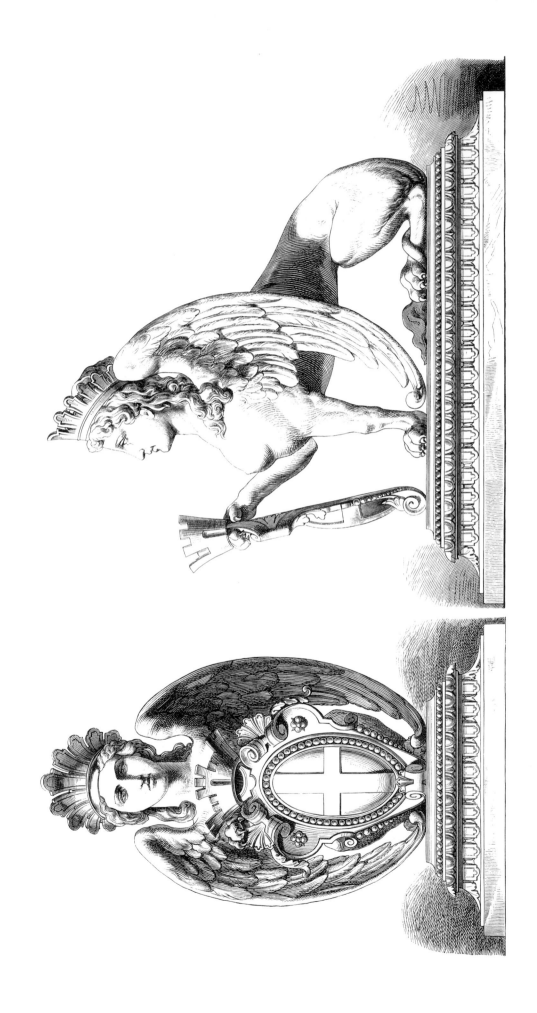

74

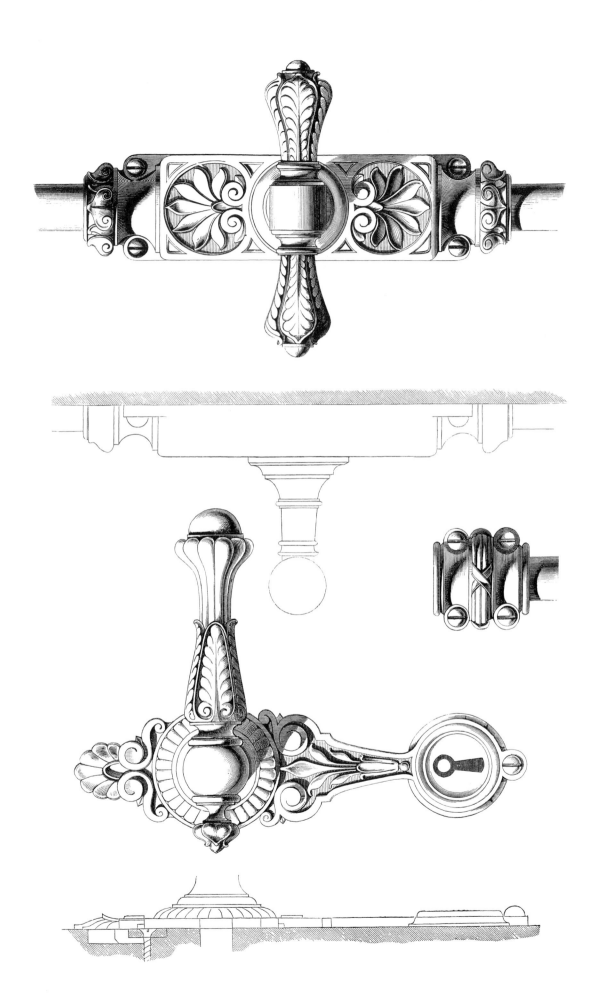

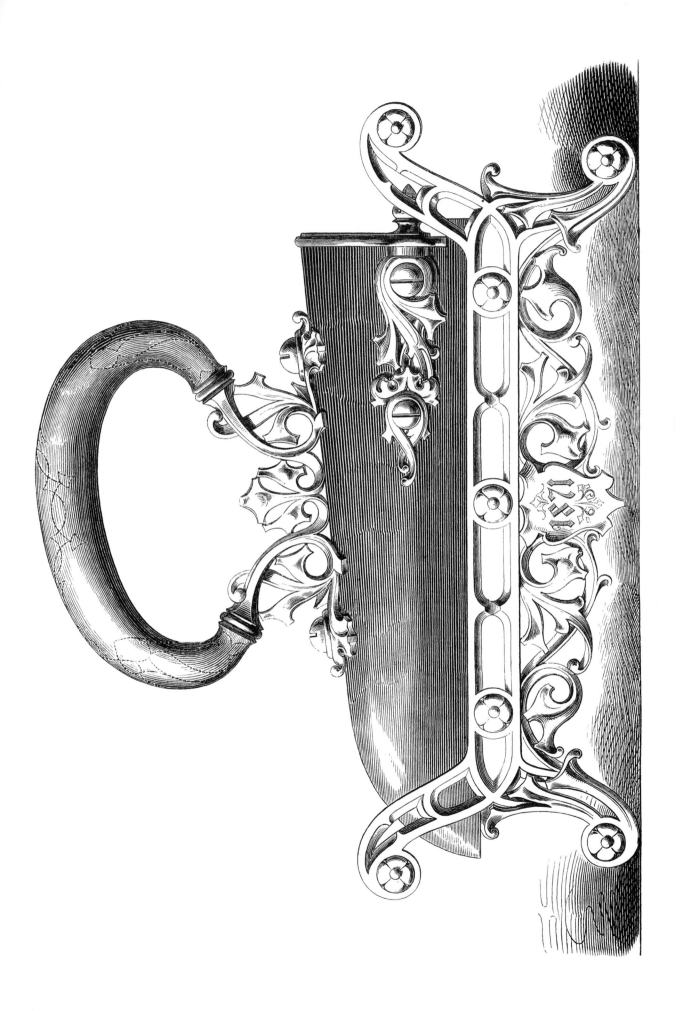

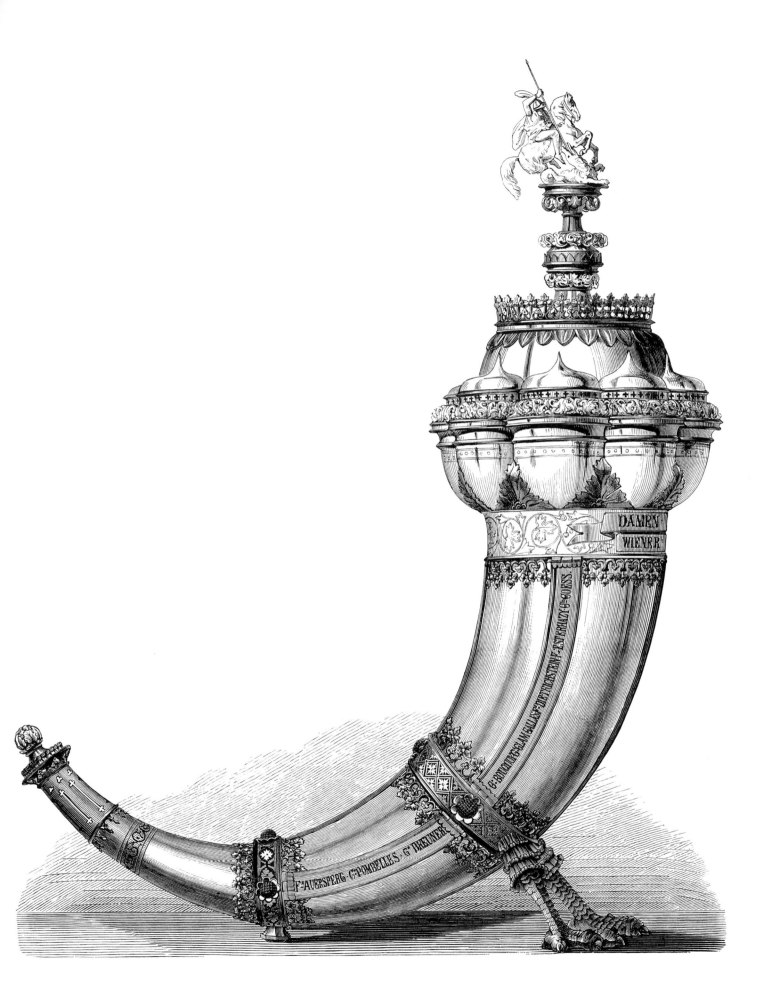

83

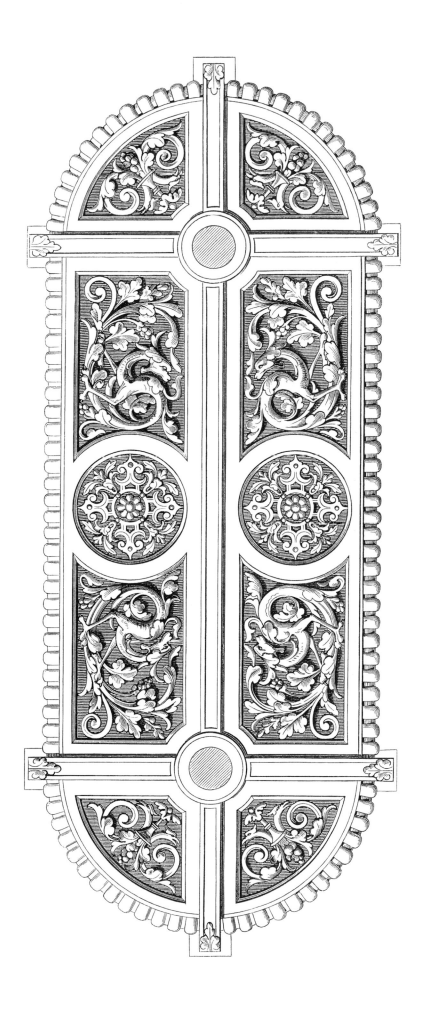

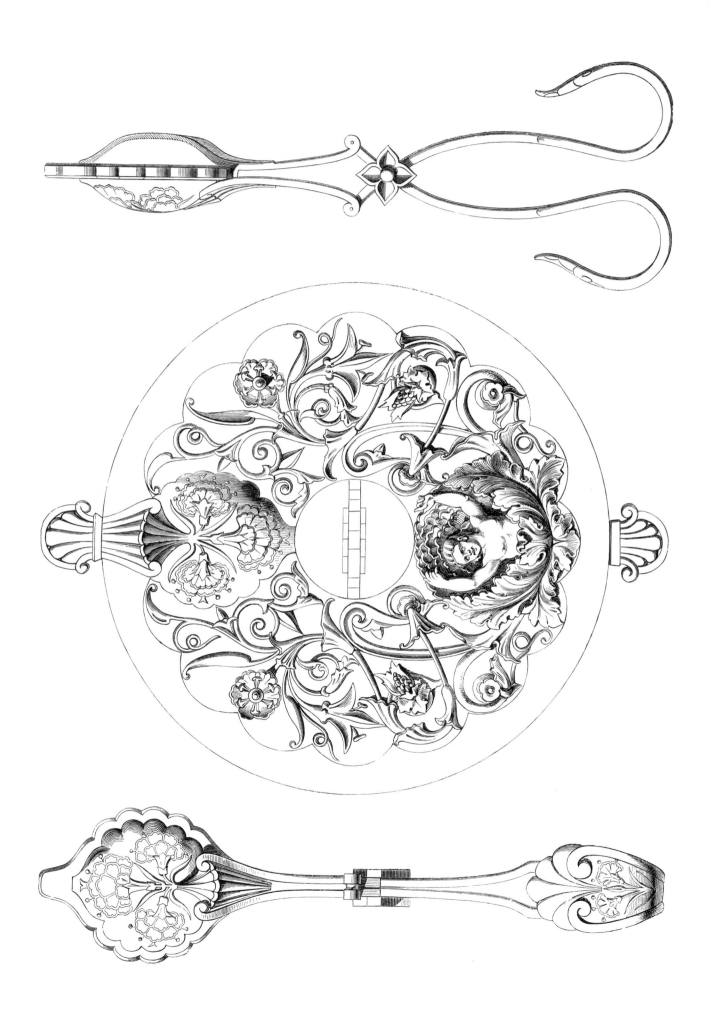

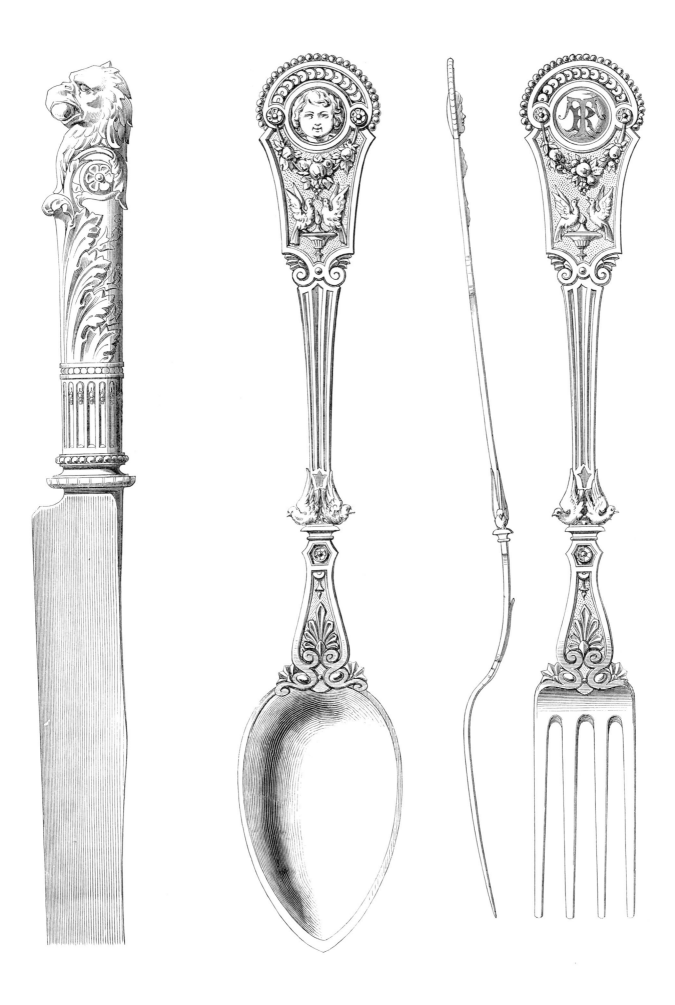

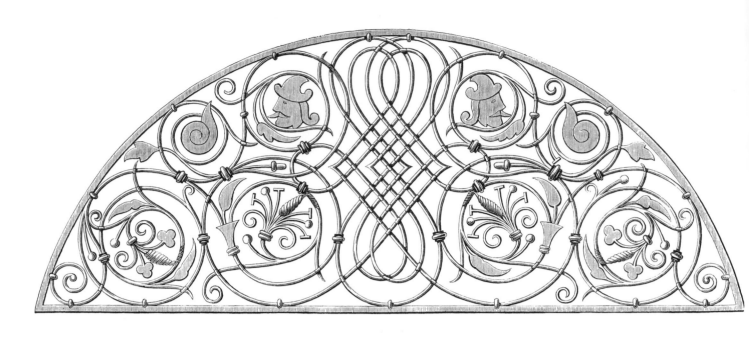

92

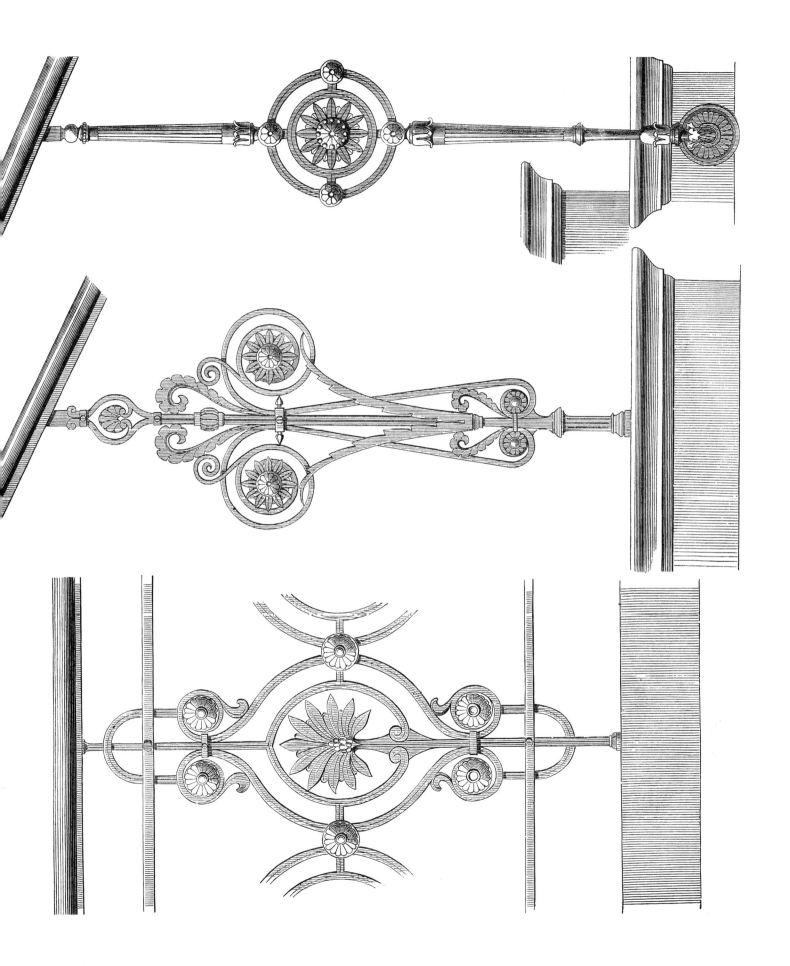

93

94

95

103

104

105

108

109

110

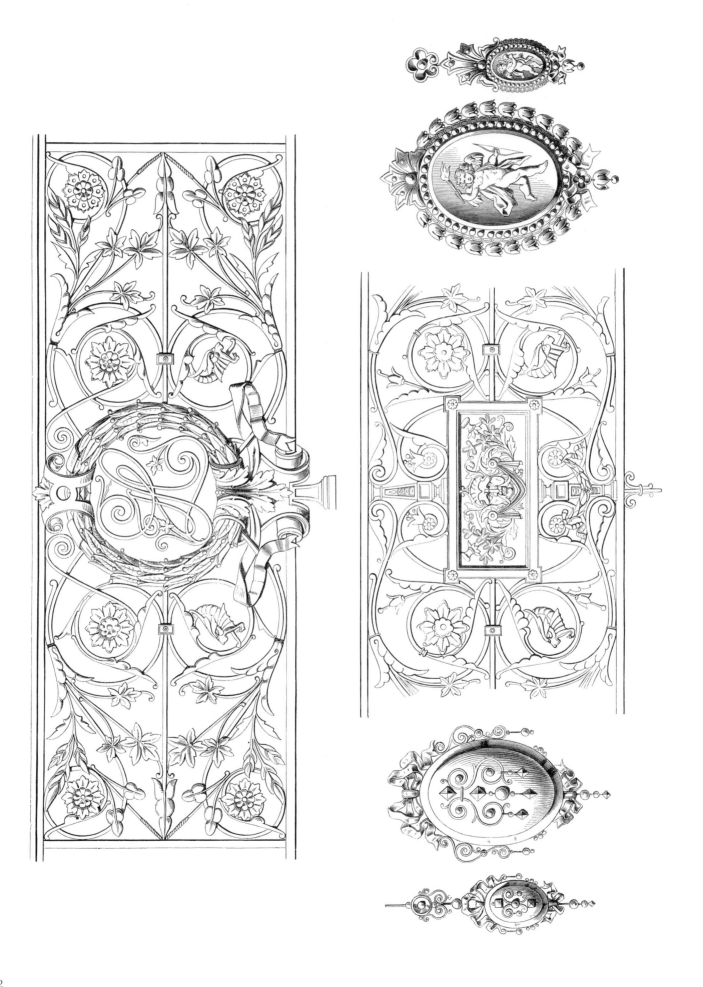

114

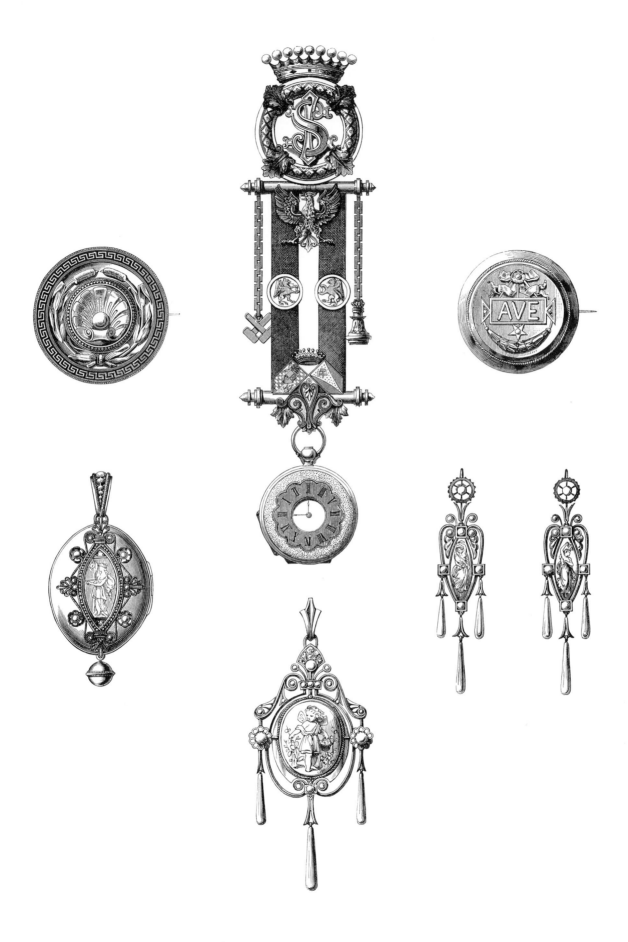

119

124

128

129

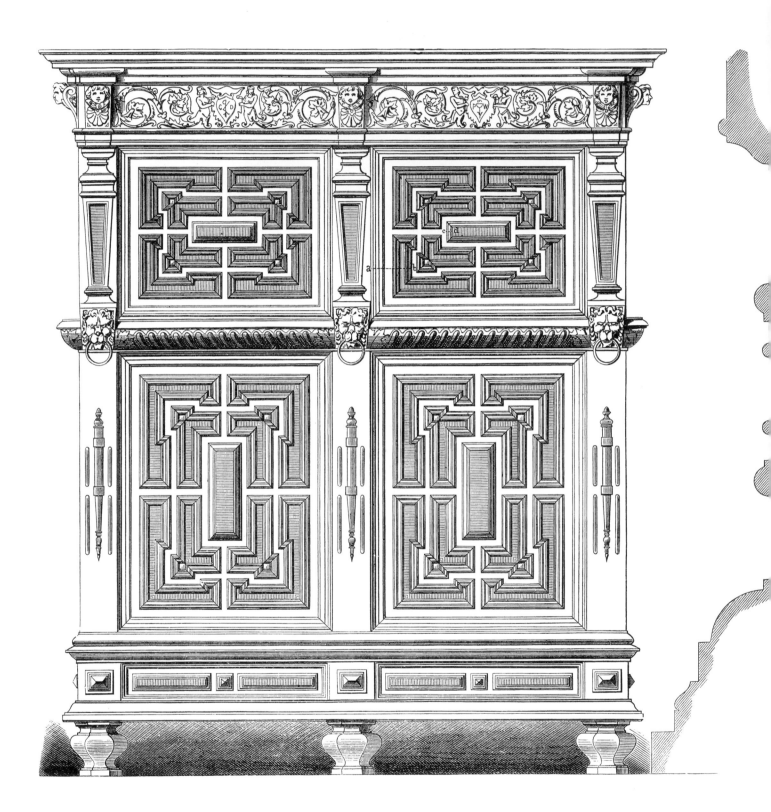

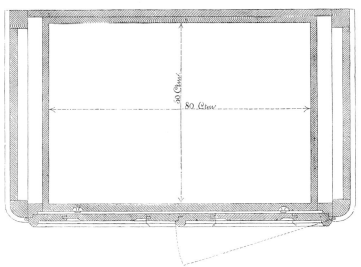

50 Ctm.

80 Ctm.

132

133

134

135

139

141

143

145

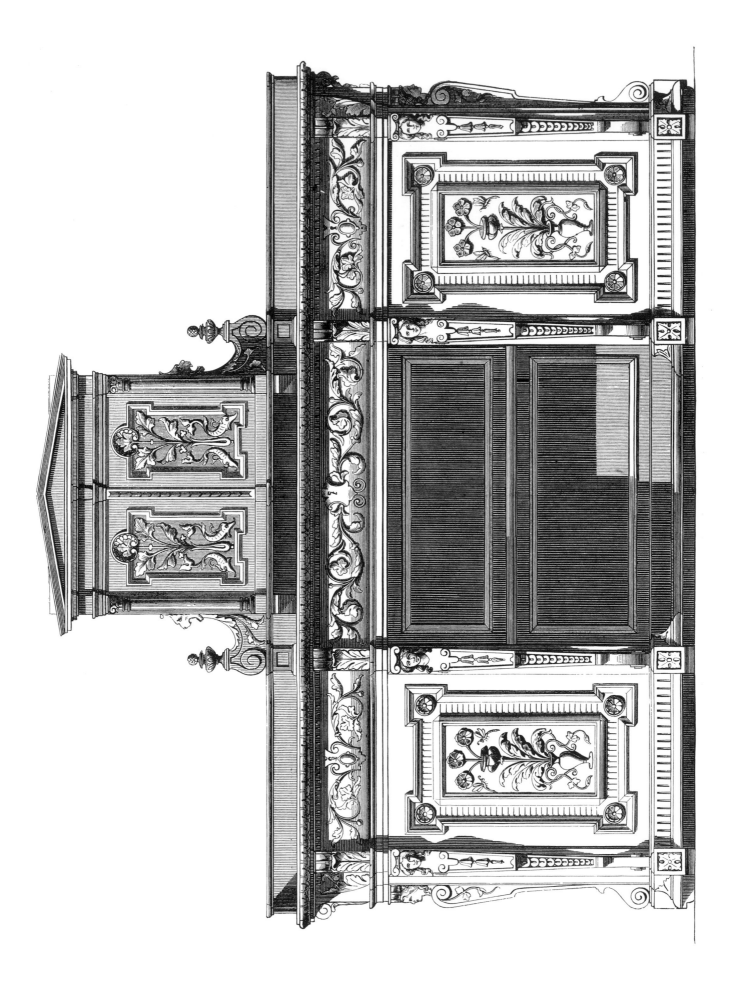

146

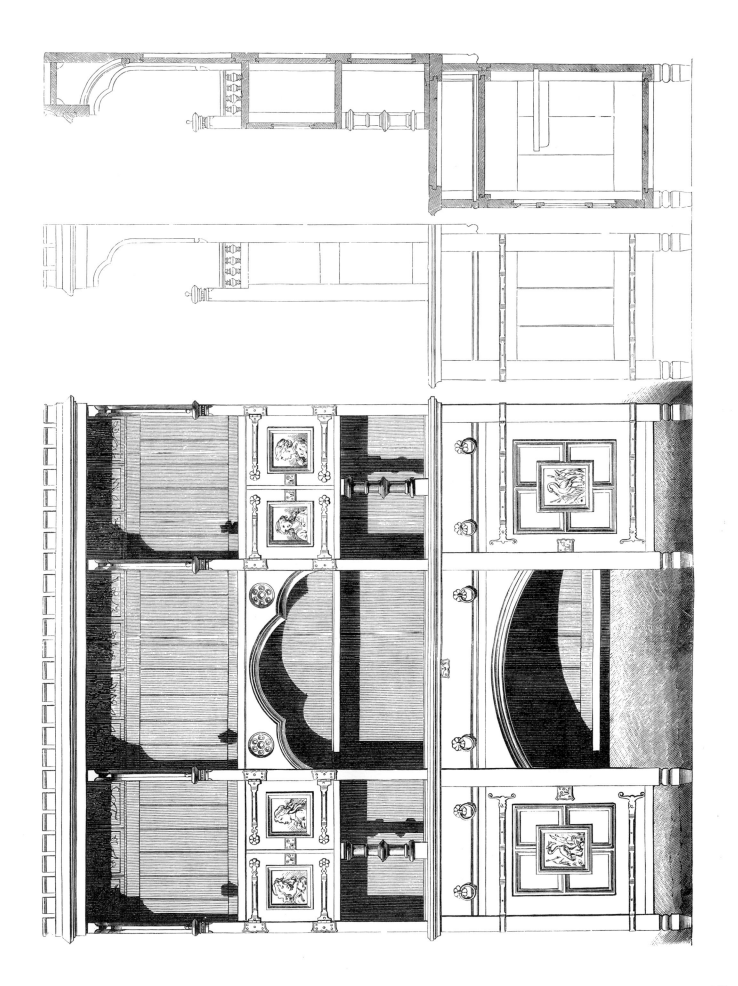

149

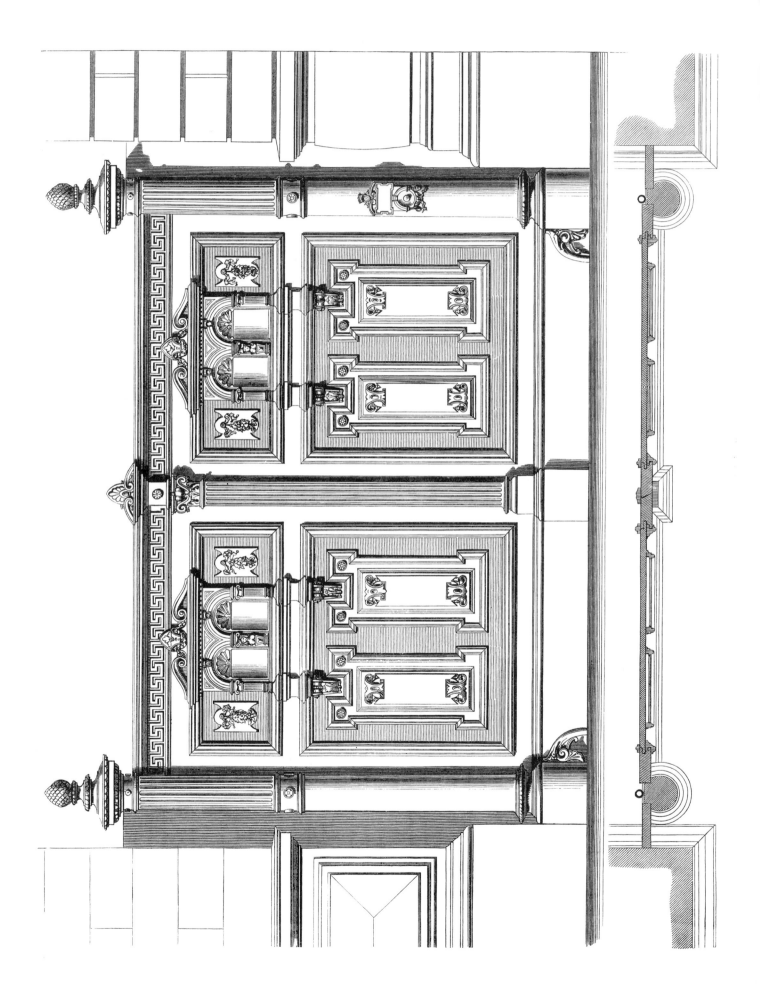

150

151

152

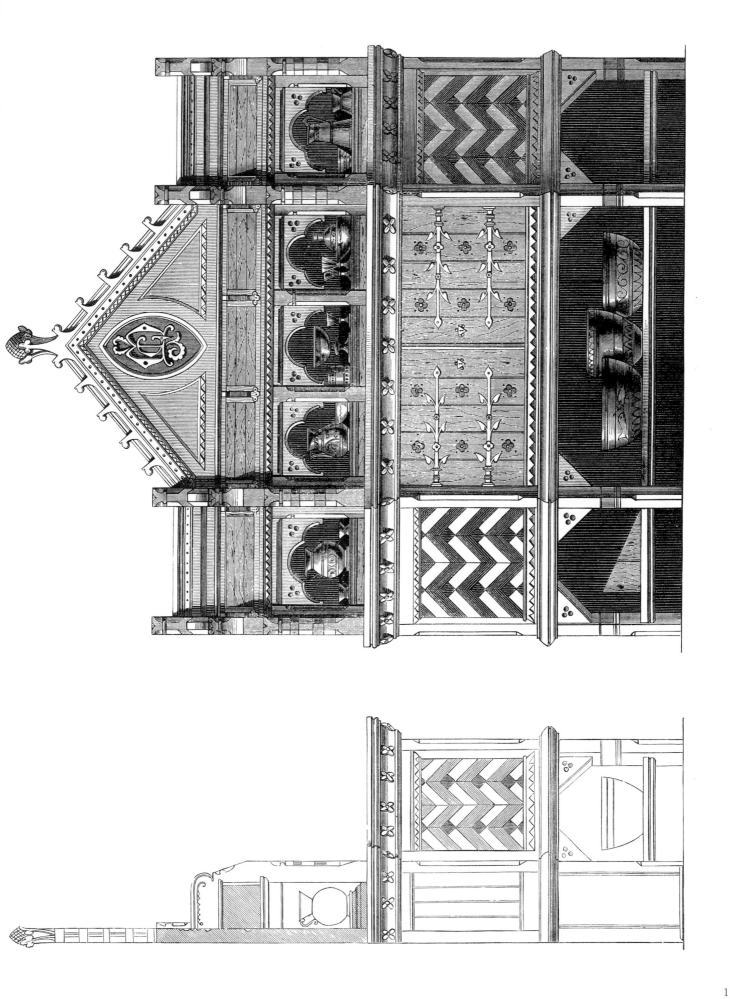

153

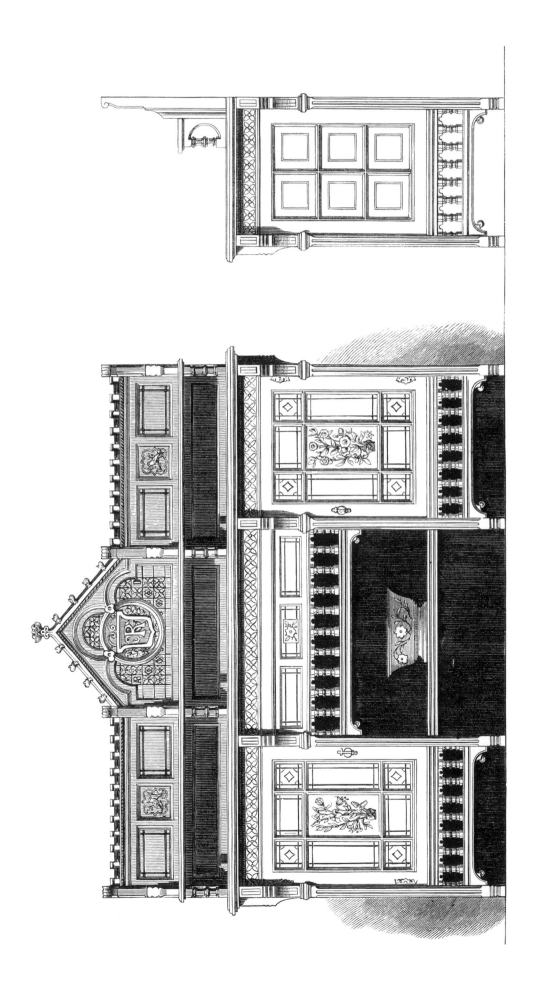

154

155

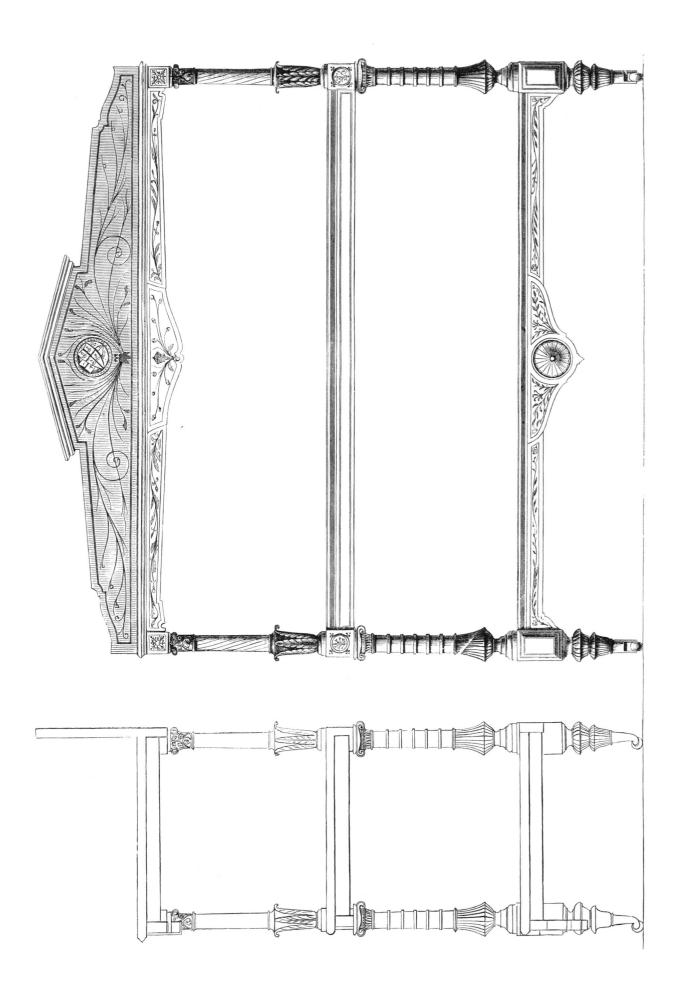

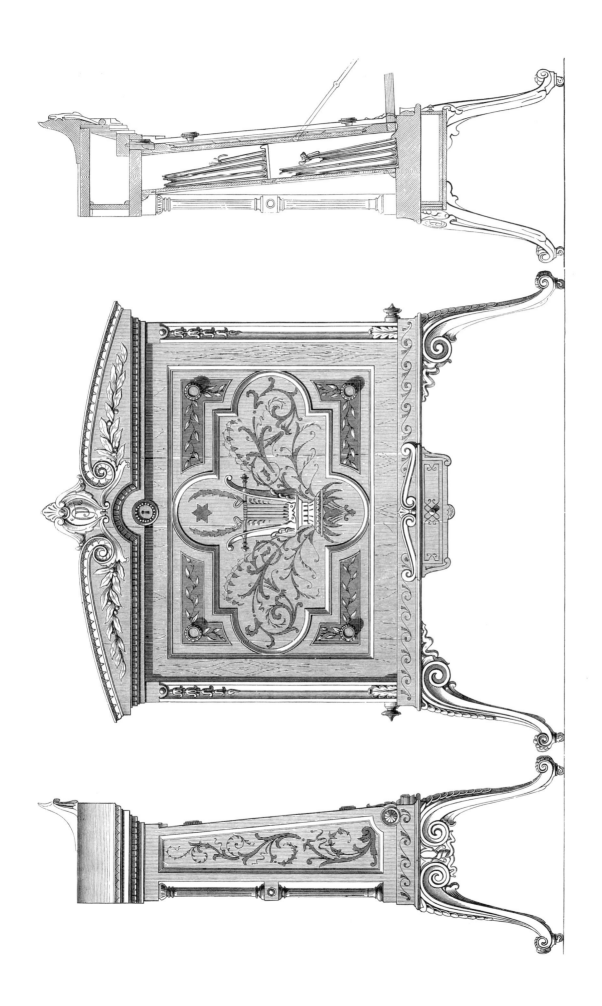

157

159

161

163

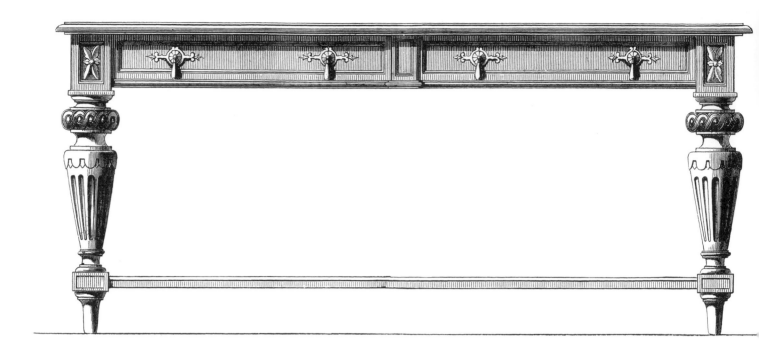

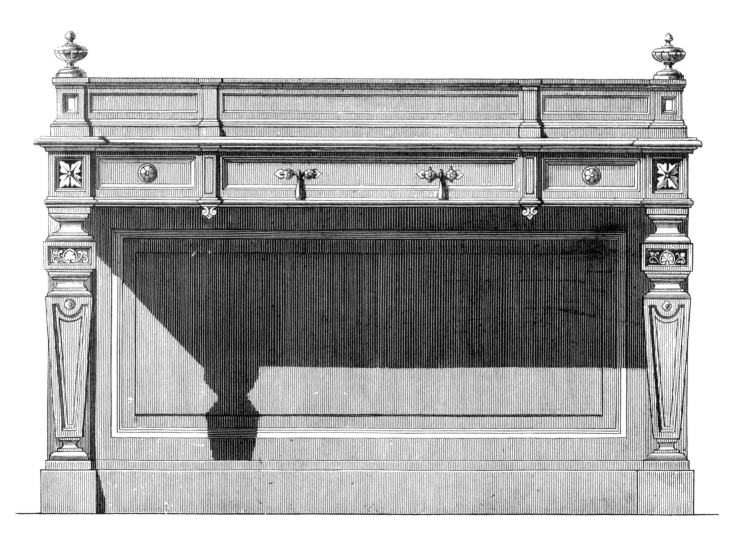

170

172

173

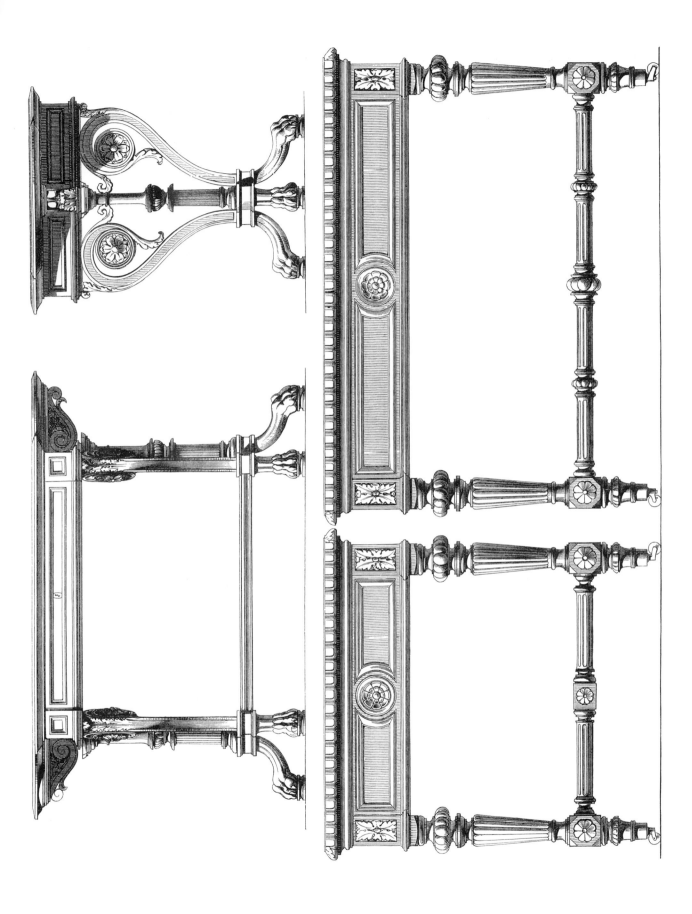

175

176

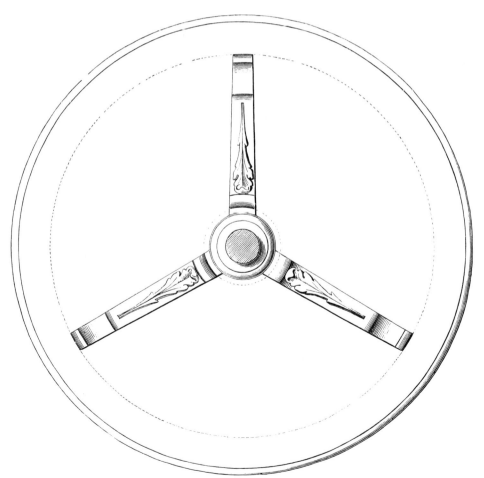

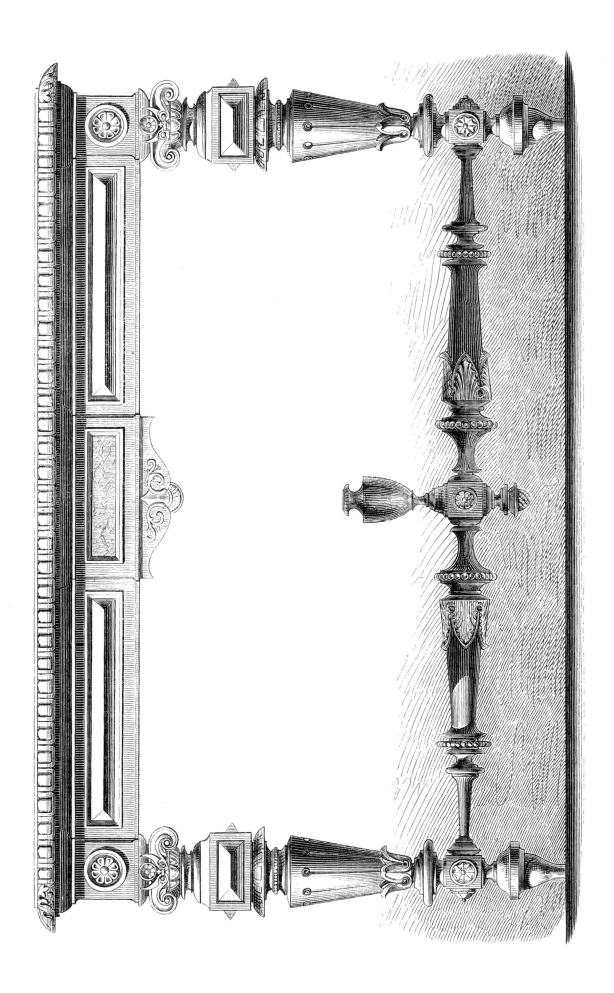

181

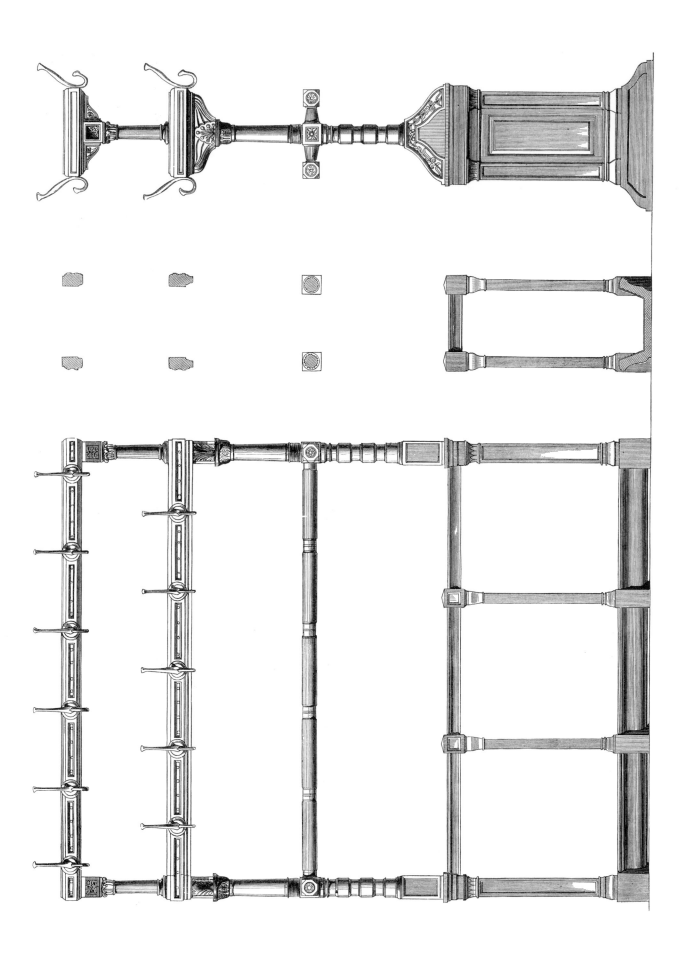

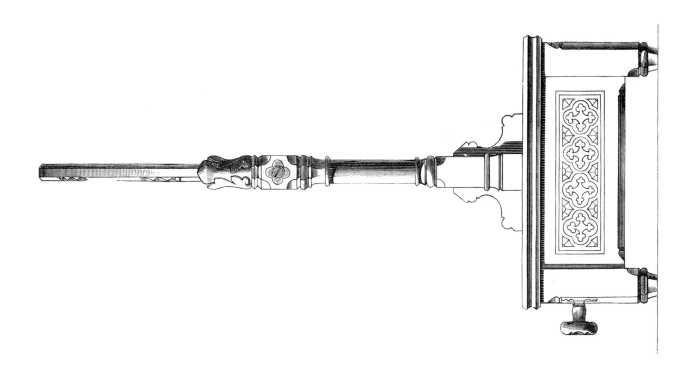

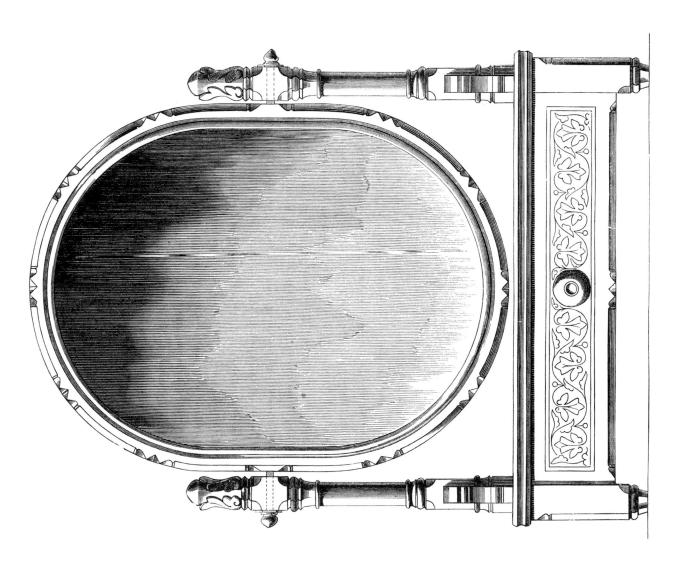

185

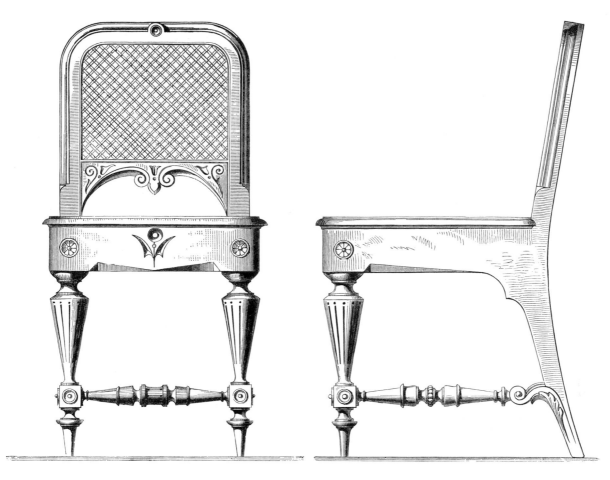

187

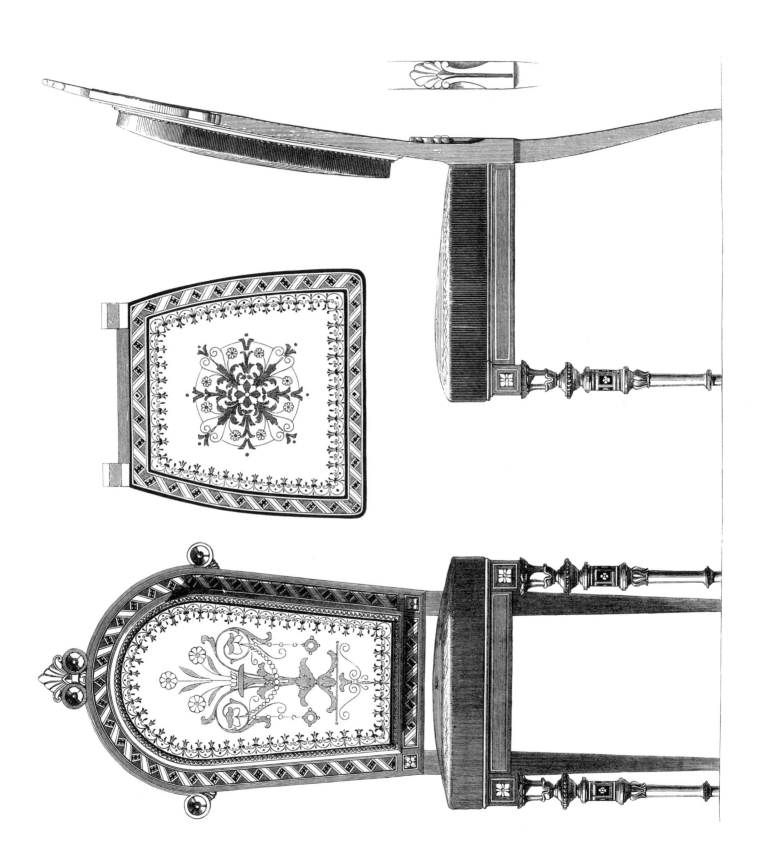

188

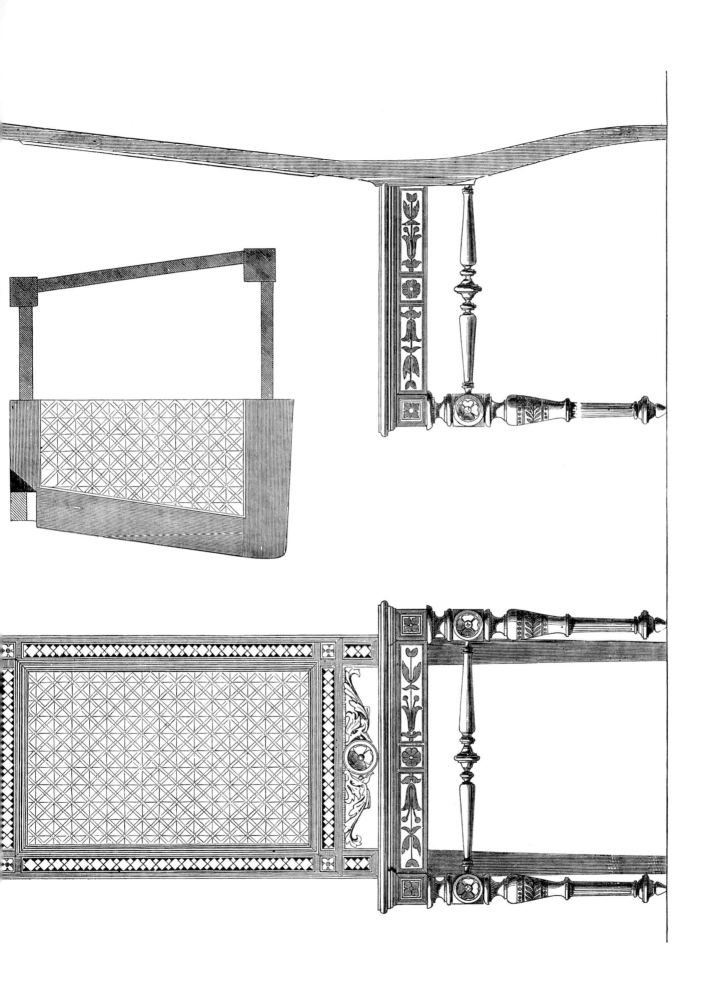

189

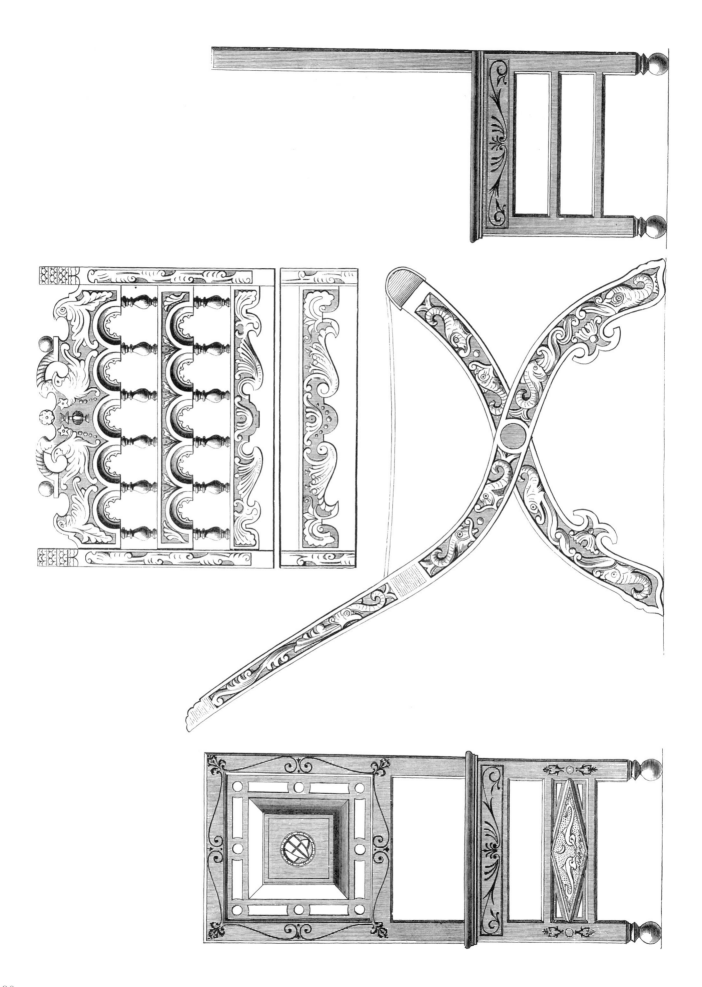

190

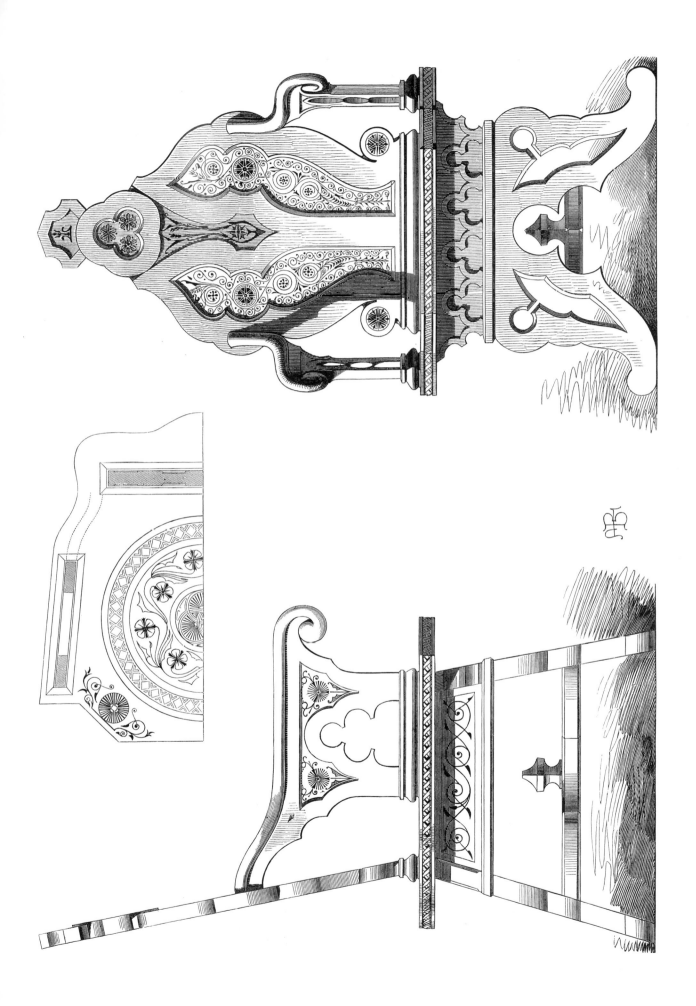

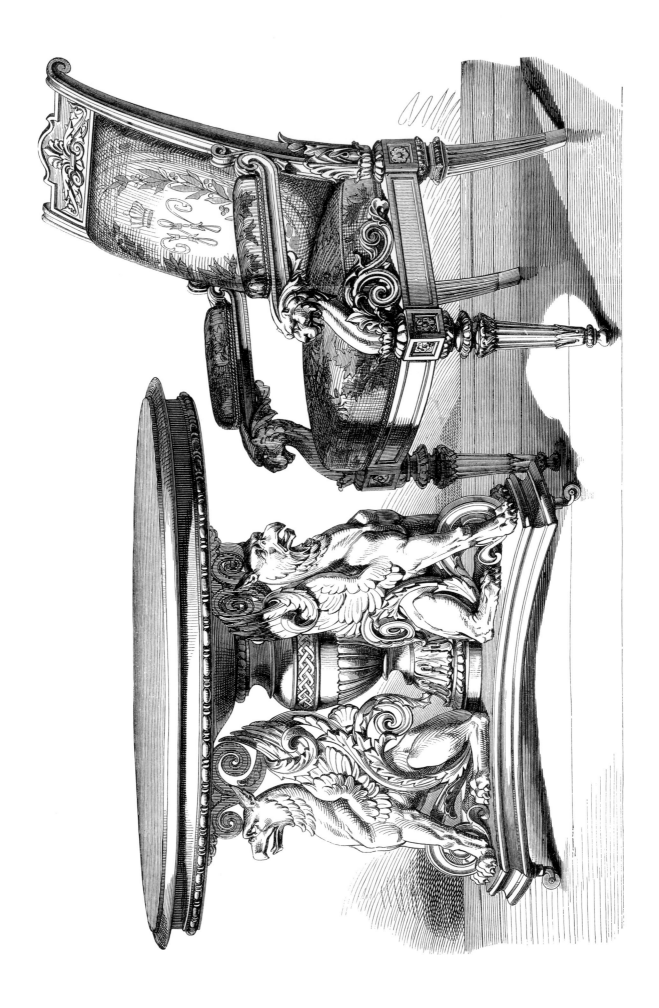

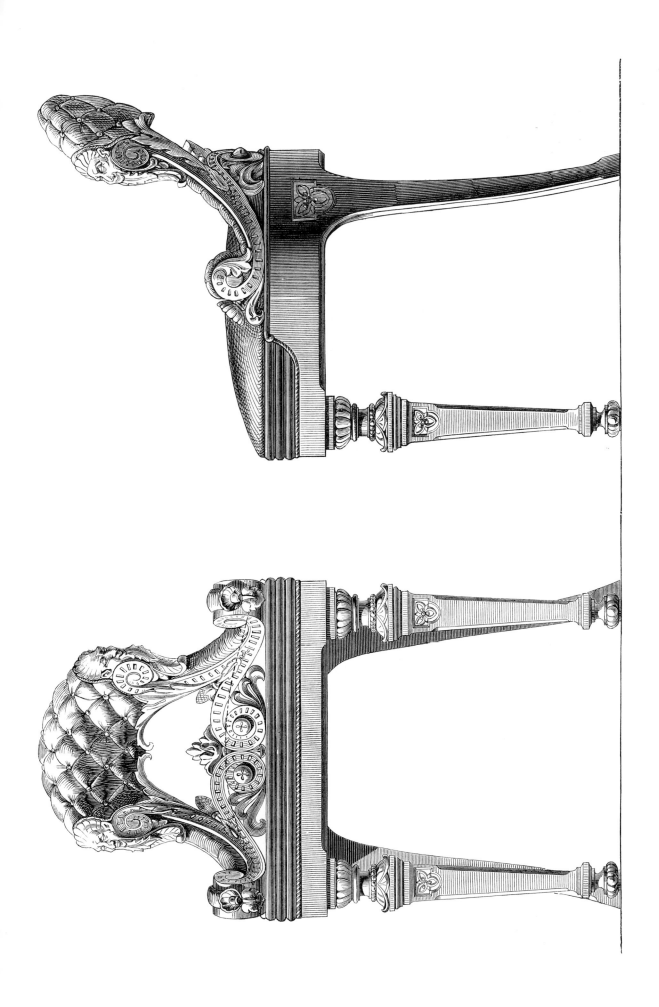

193

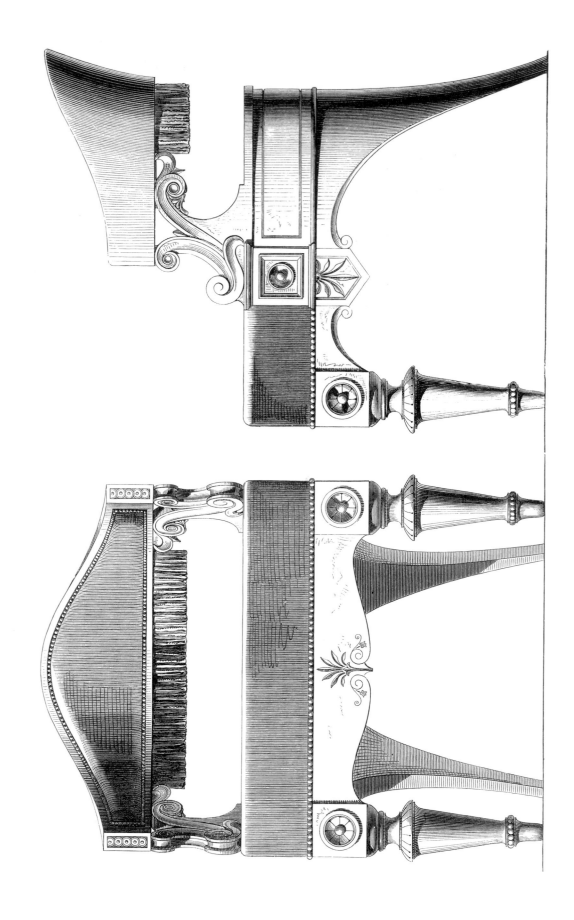

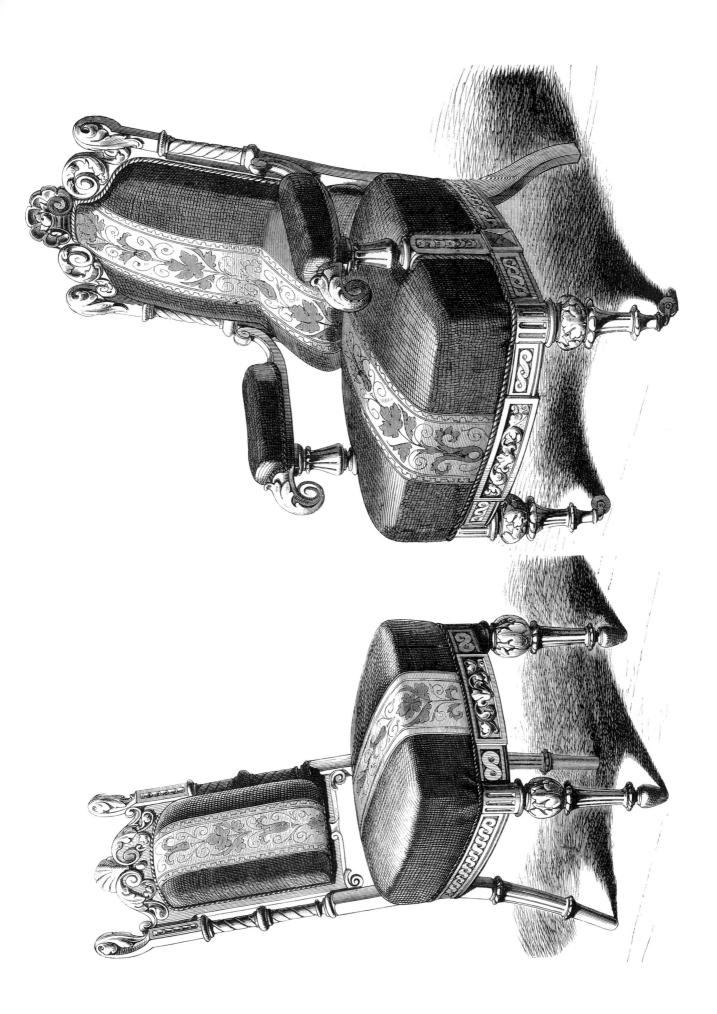

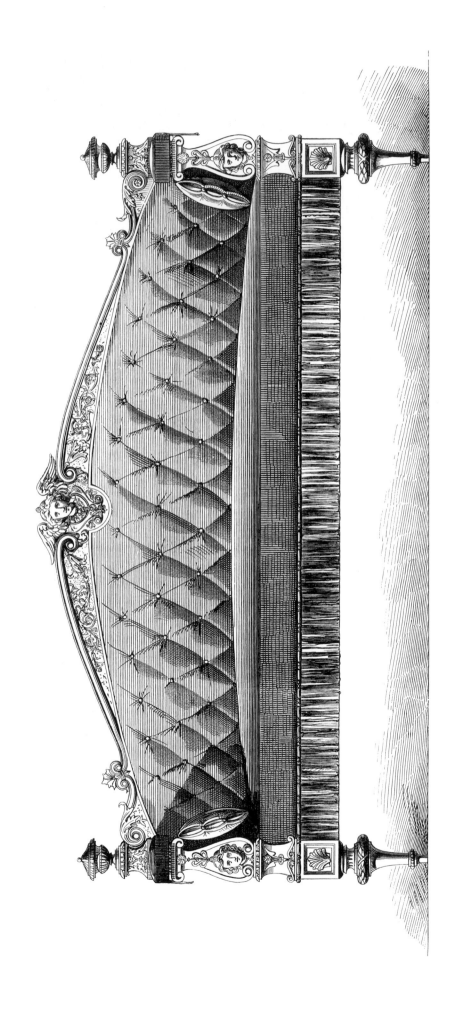

196

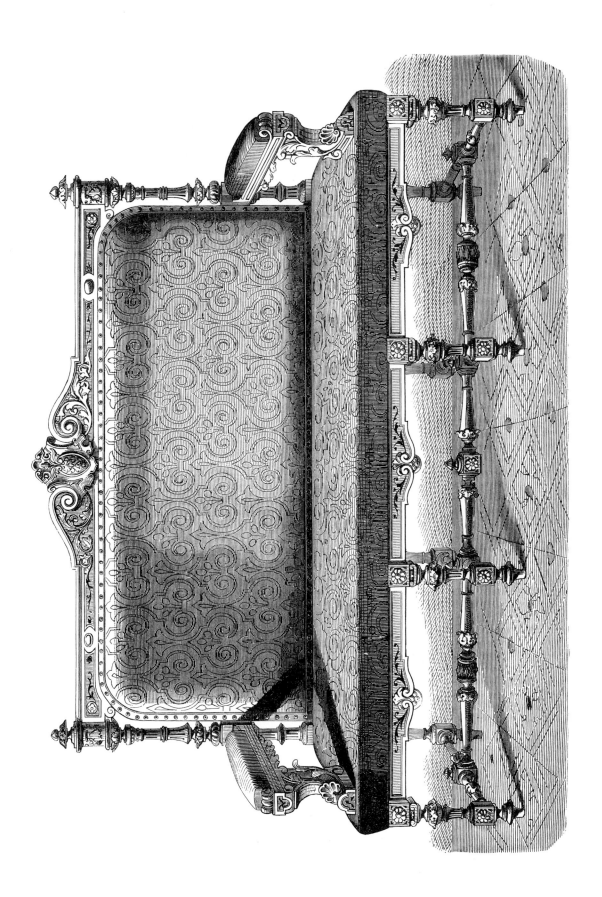

197

199

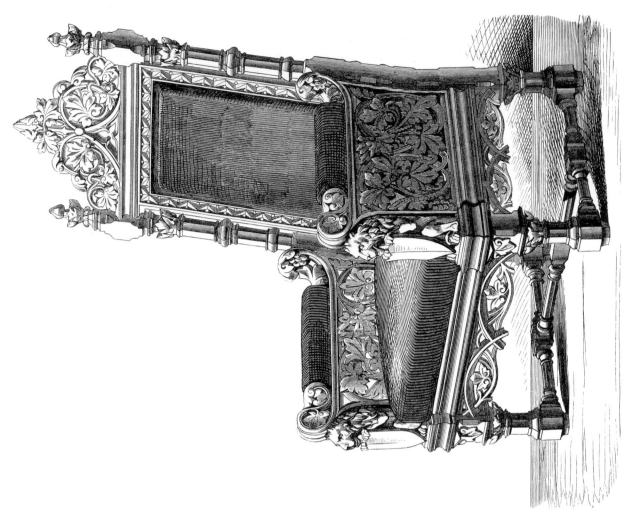

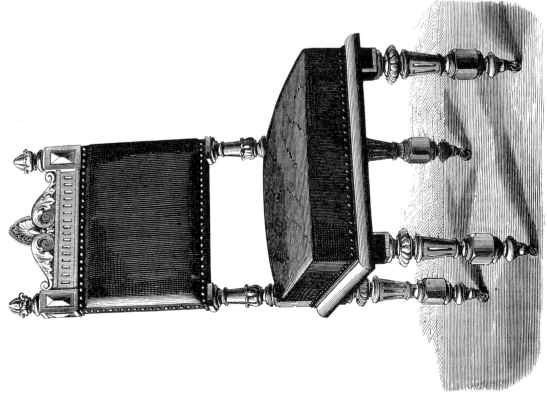

200

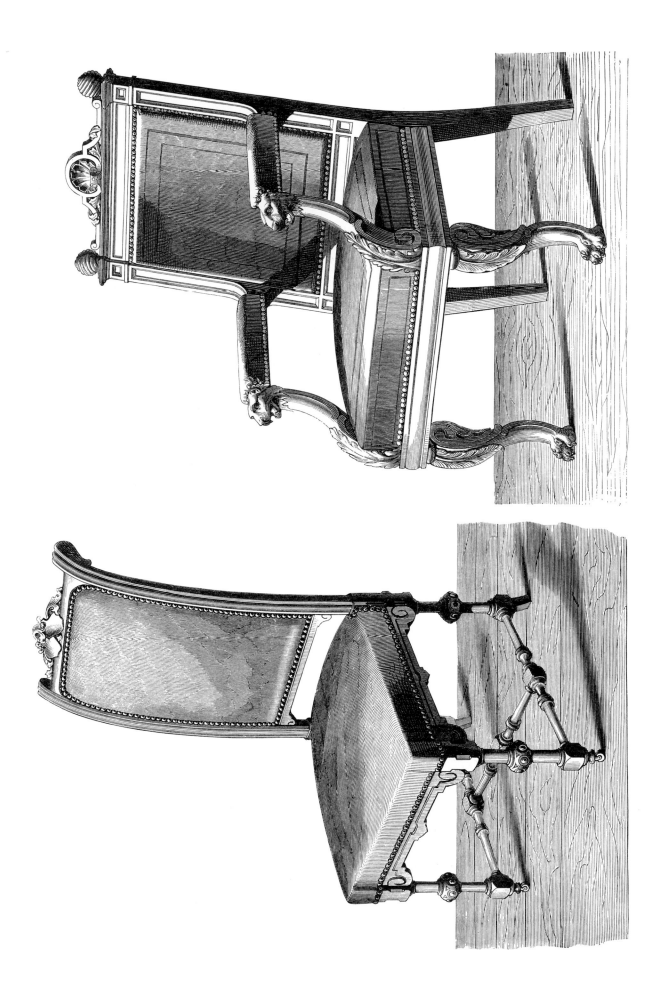

203

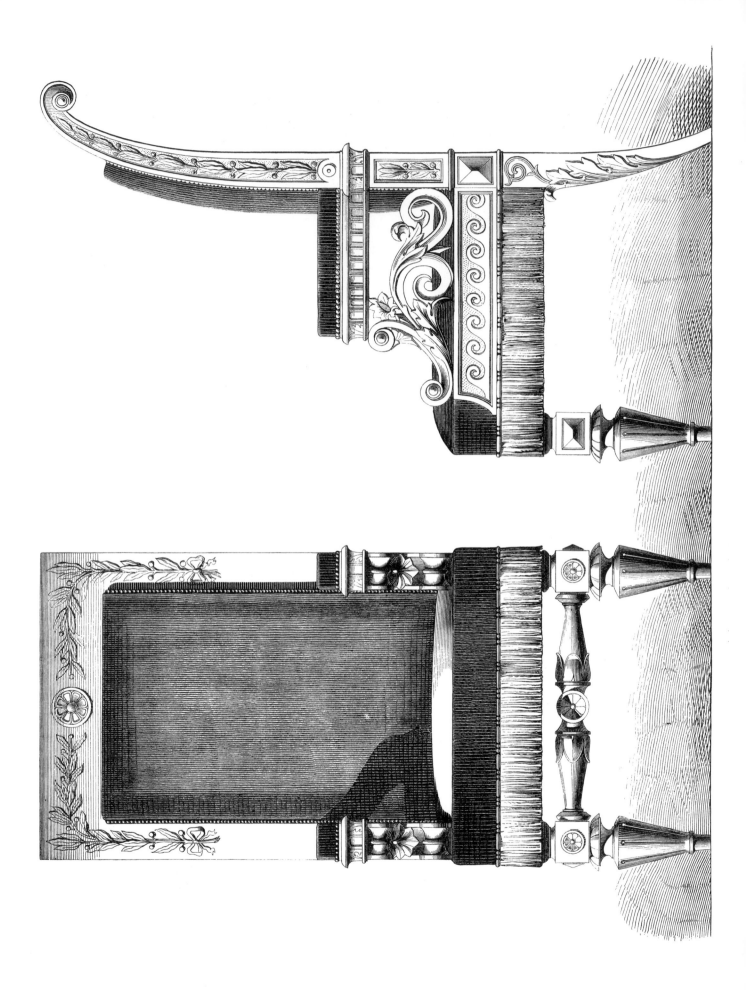

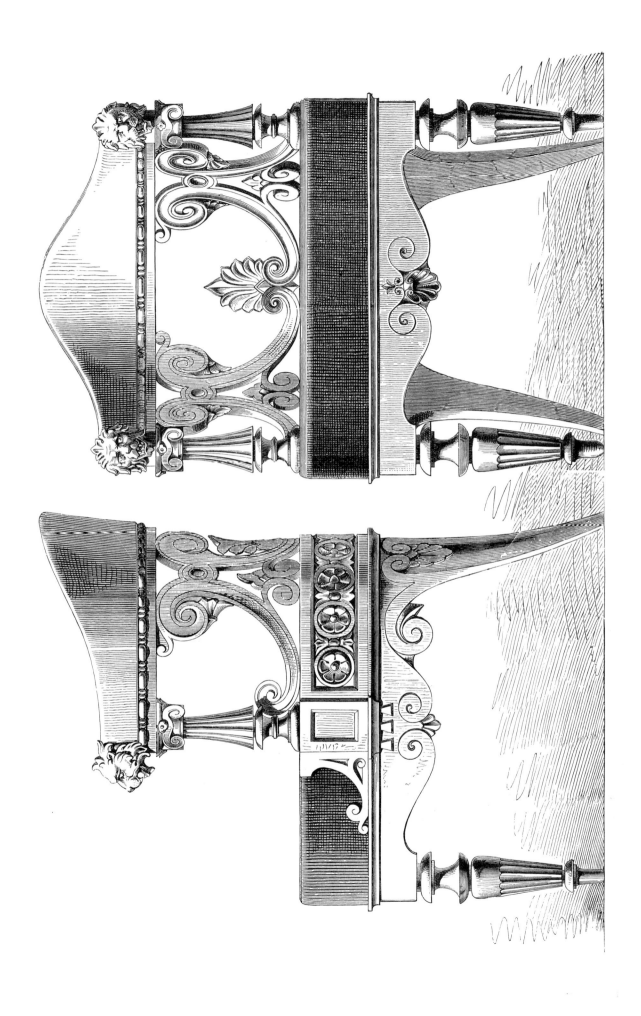

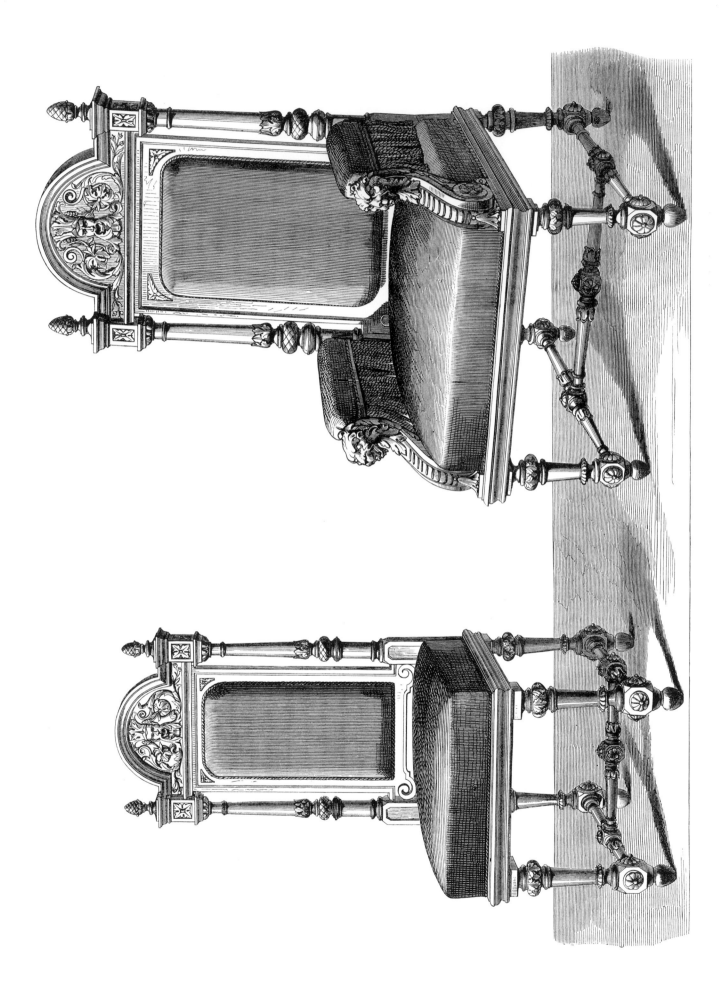

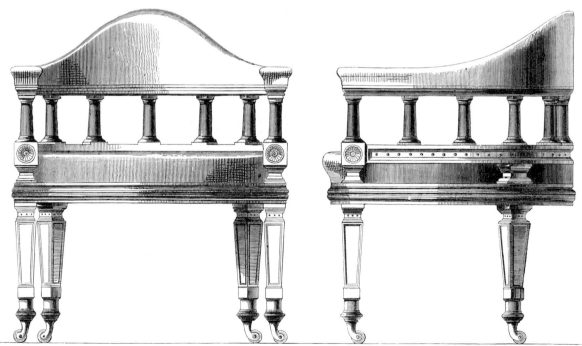

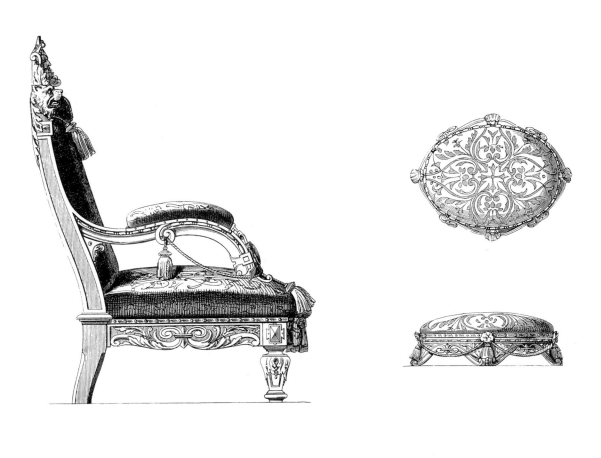

209

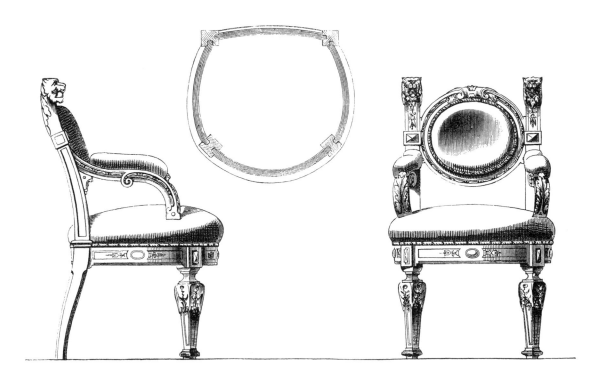

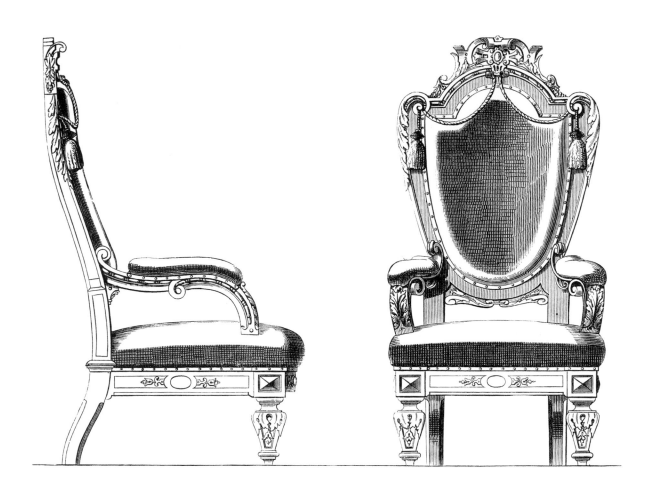

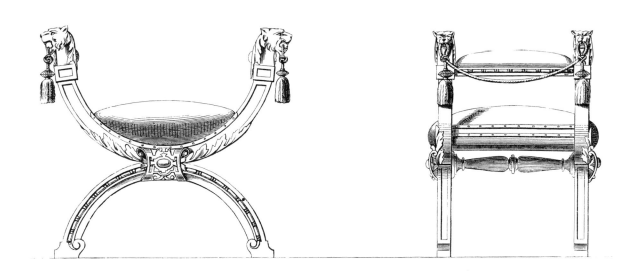

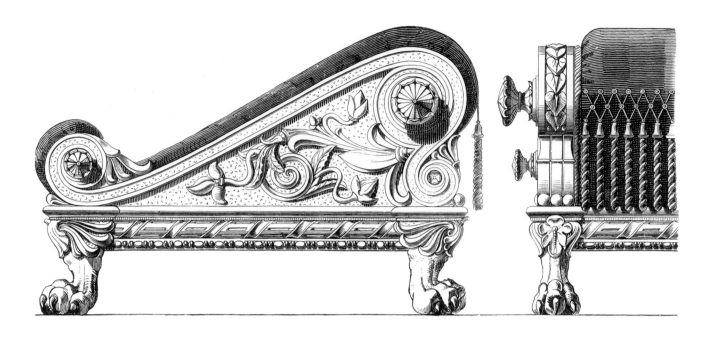

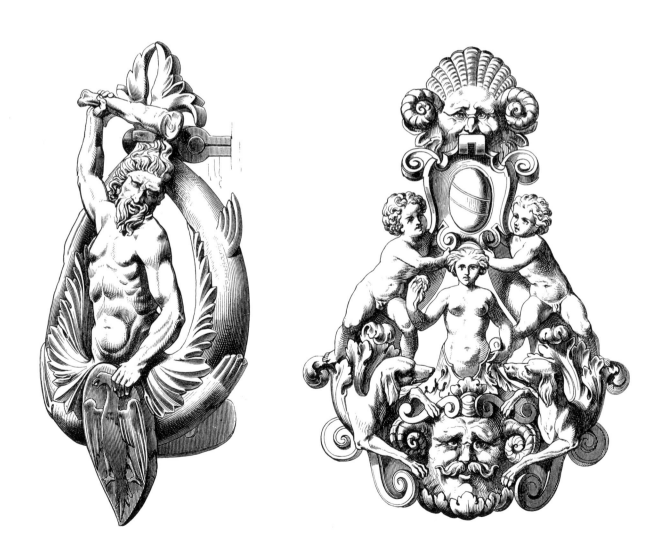

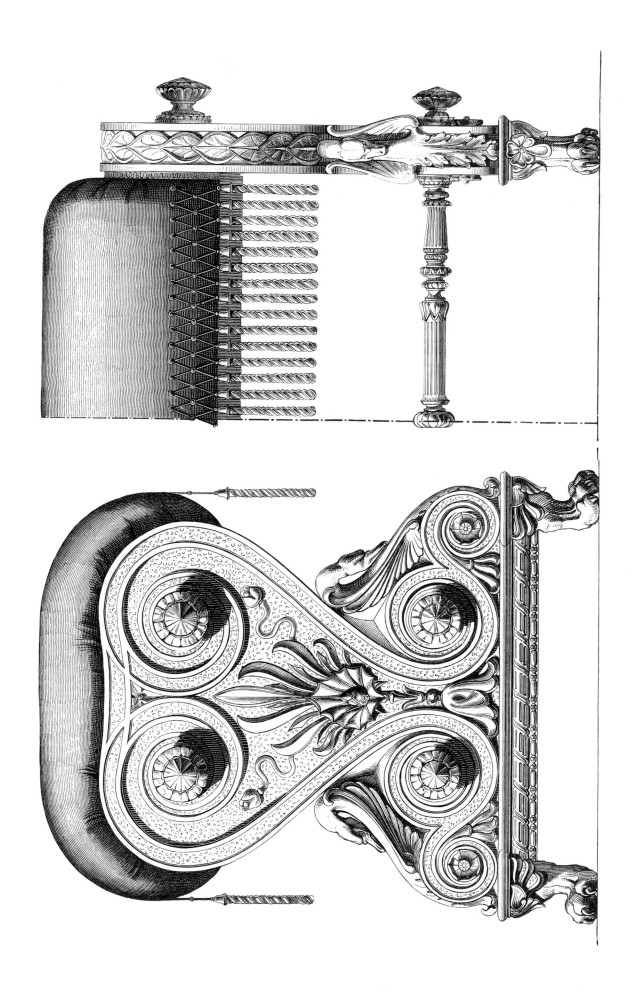

213

214

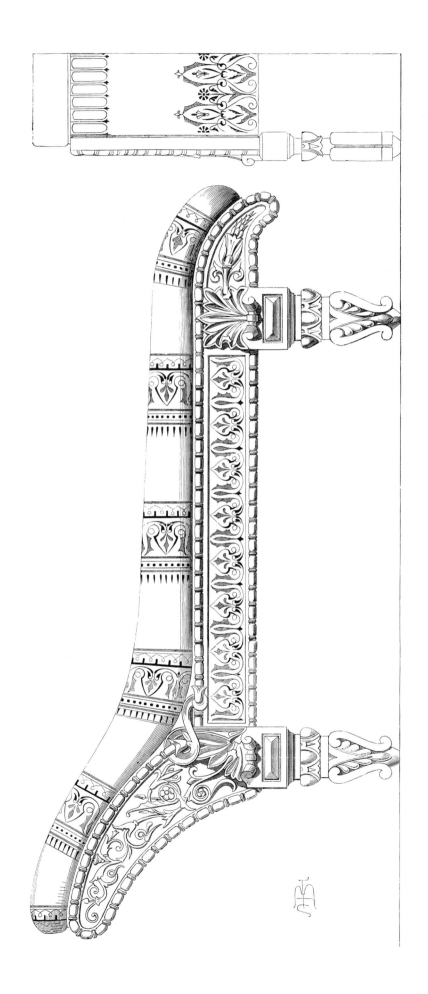

215

216

220

0 5 10   100   200 Ctm.

221

222

223

225

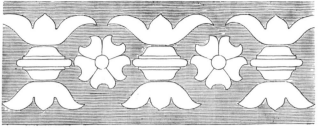

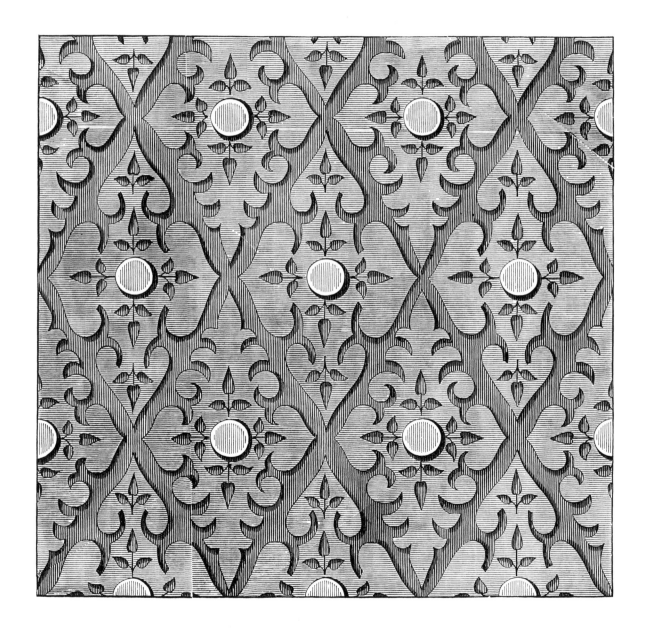

230

231

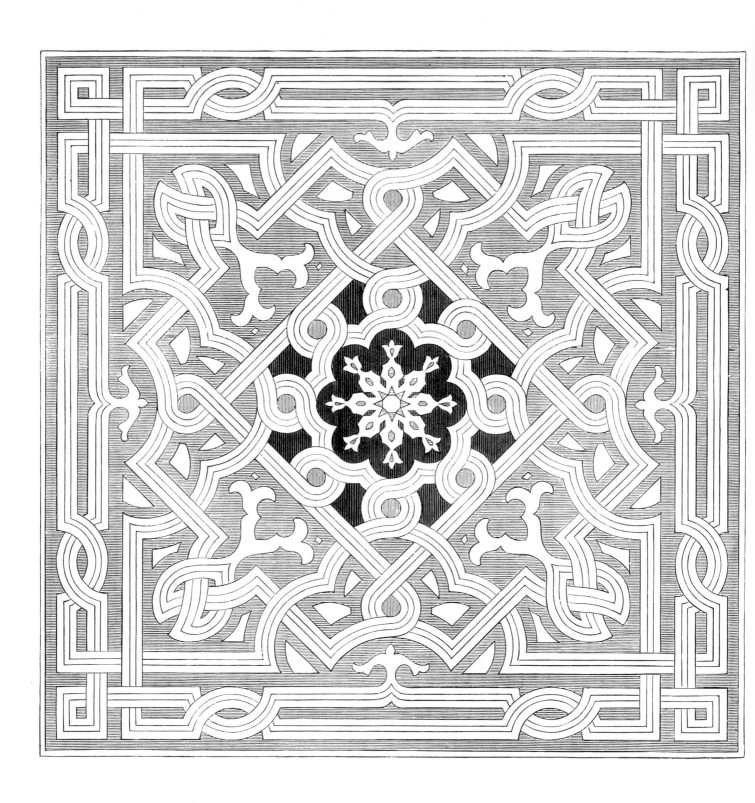

236

238

239

241

242

243

244

245

246

Nr. 10.

249

252

253

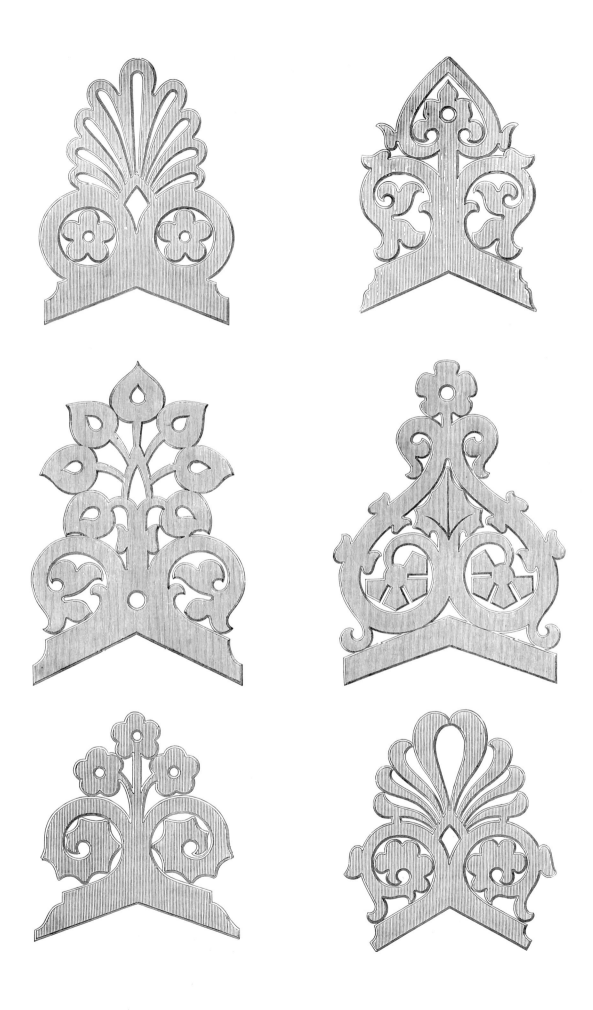

255

257

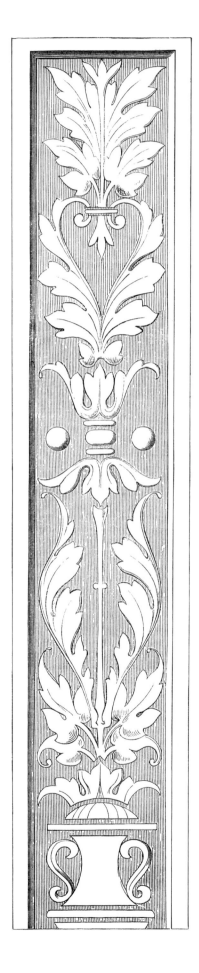

258

259

261

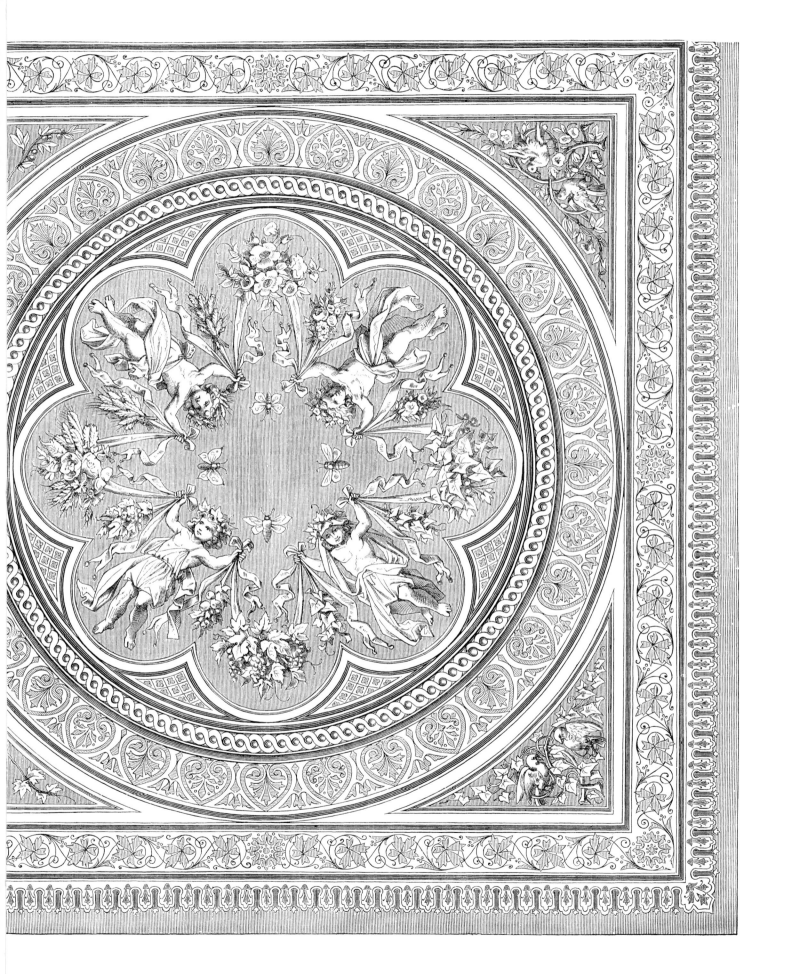

265

273

275

276

278

279

283

285

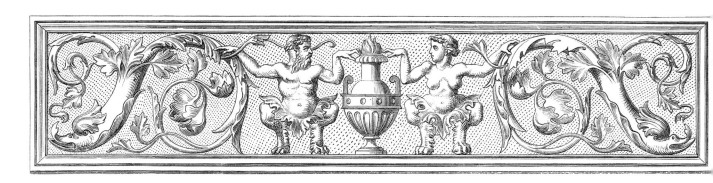

289

290

291

293

294

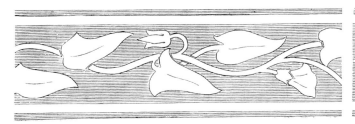

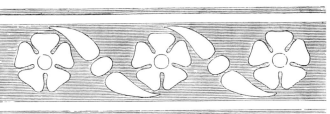

296

299

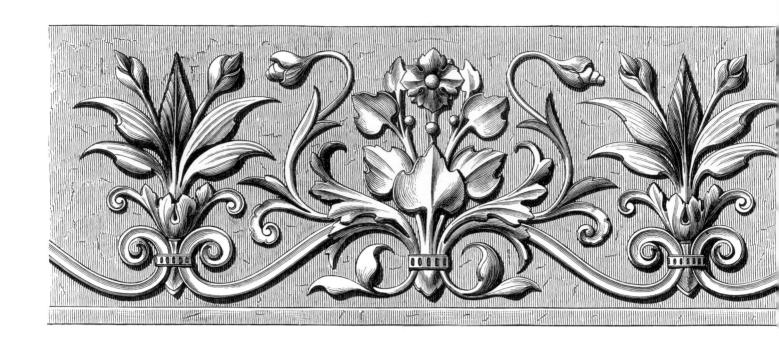

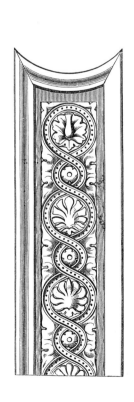

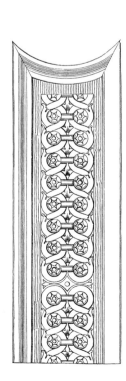

303

307

Nr. 13.

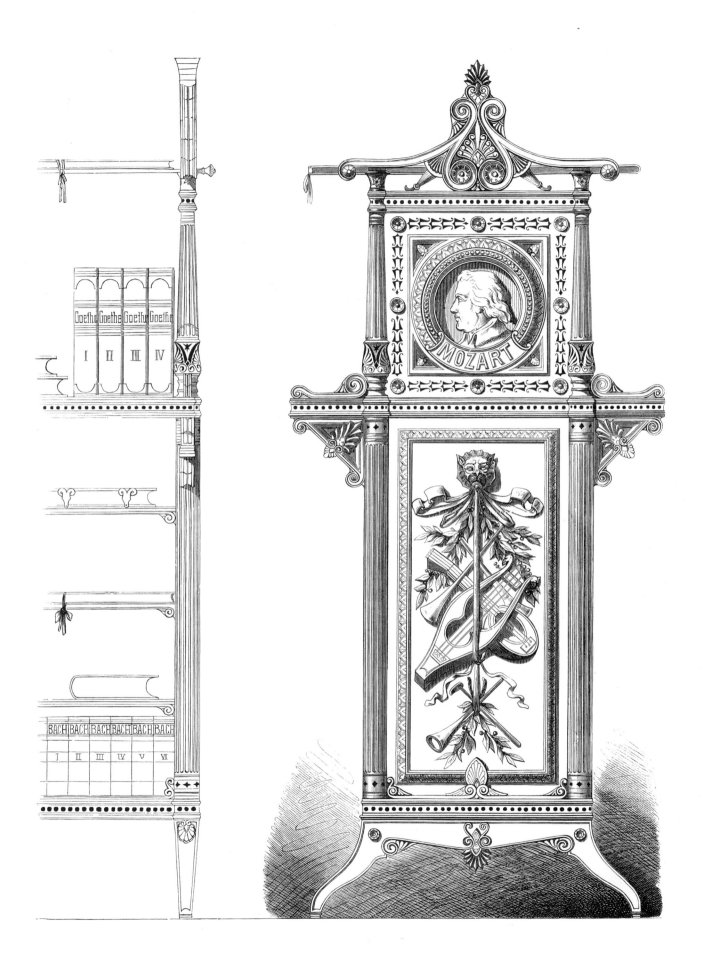

312

313

315

316

317

318

319

320

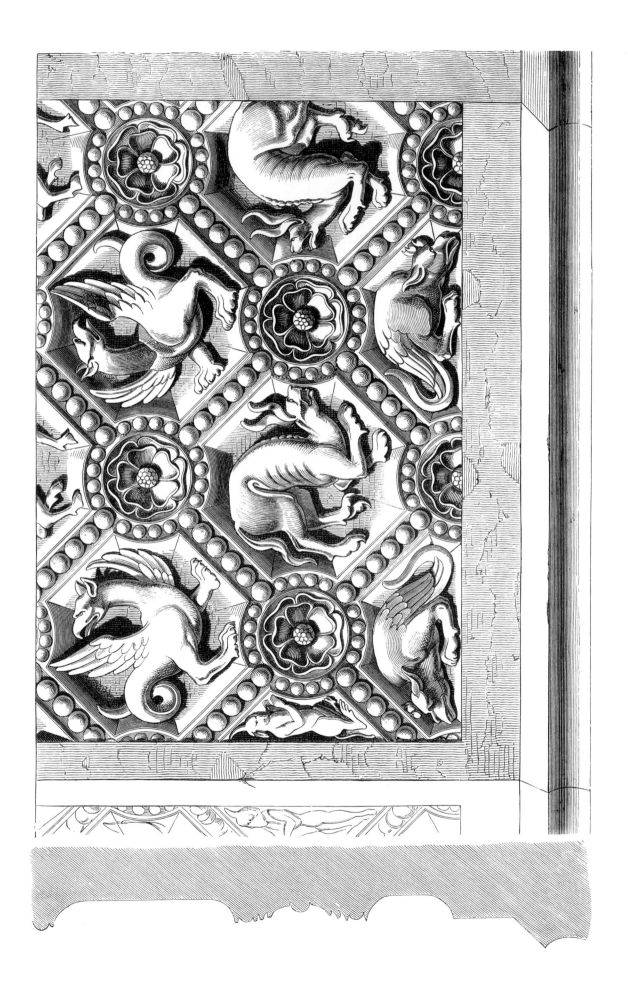

328

329

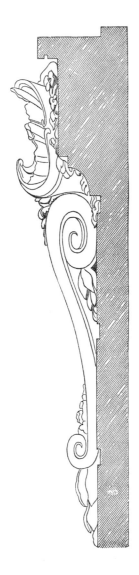

330

331

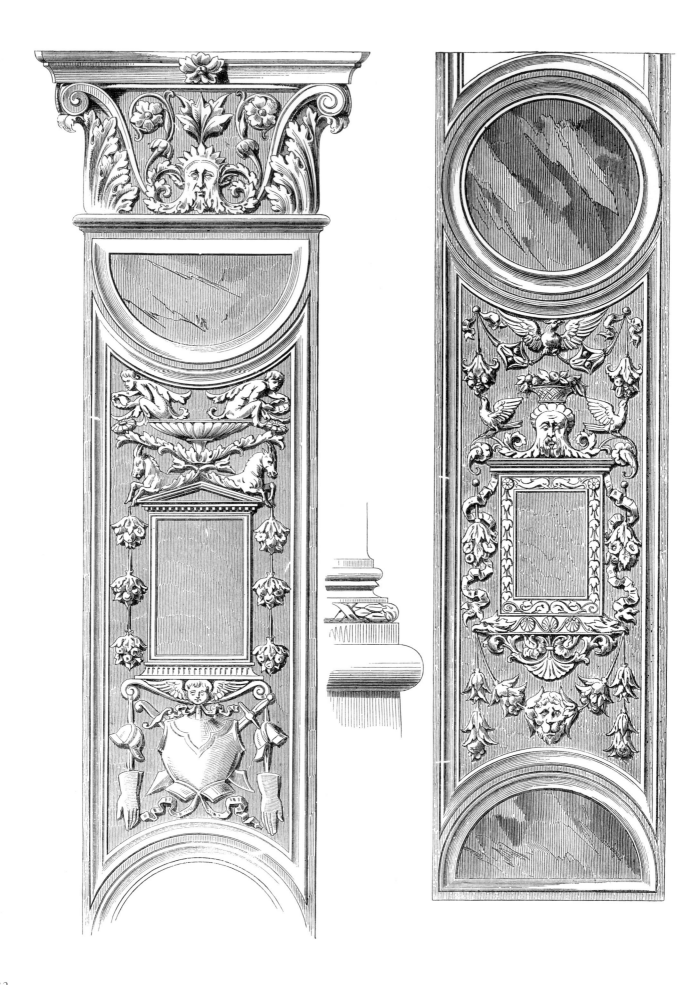

334

337

338

339

342

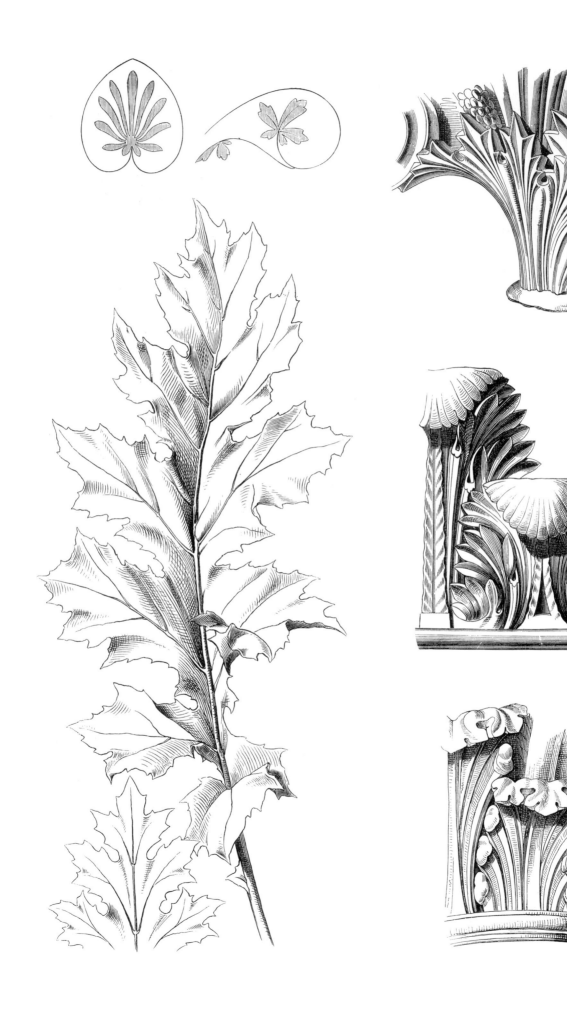

347

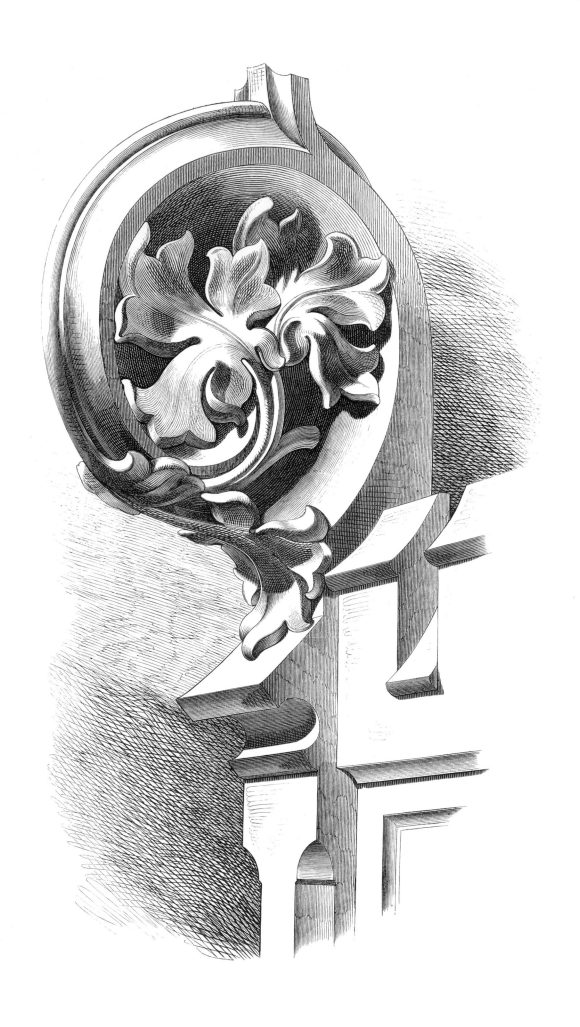

350

351

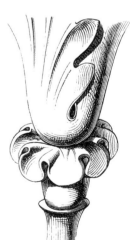

353

354

355

357

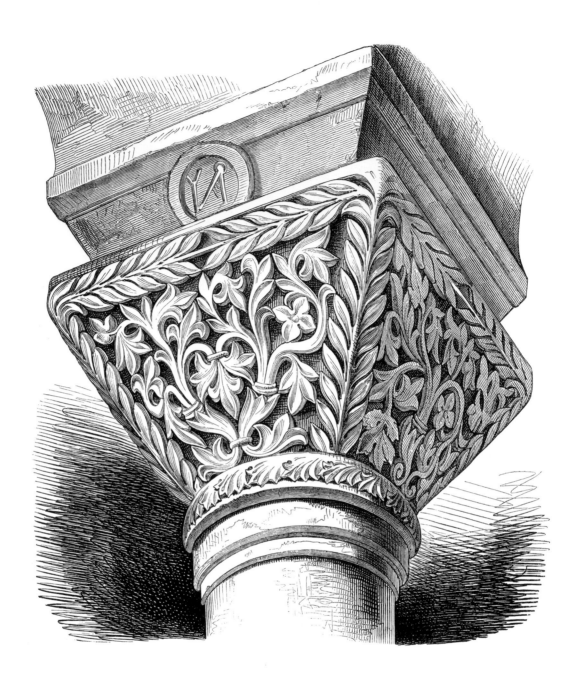

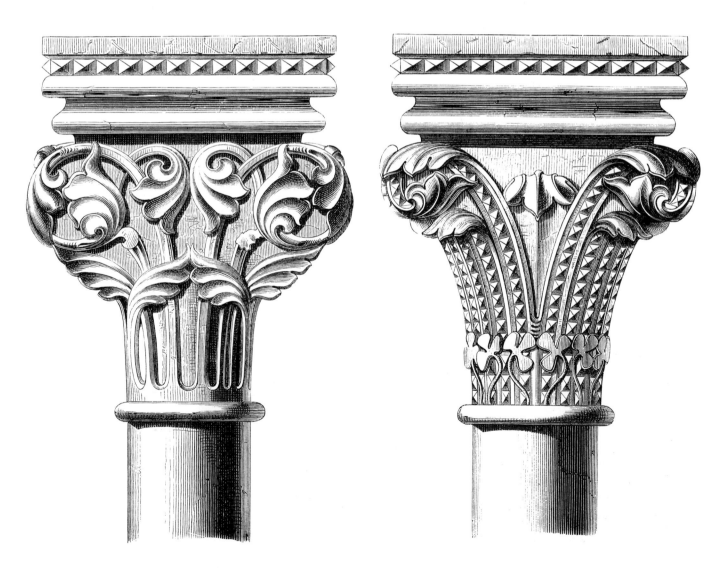

359

361

362

363

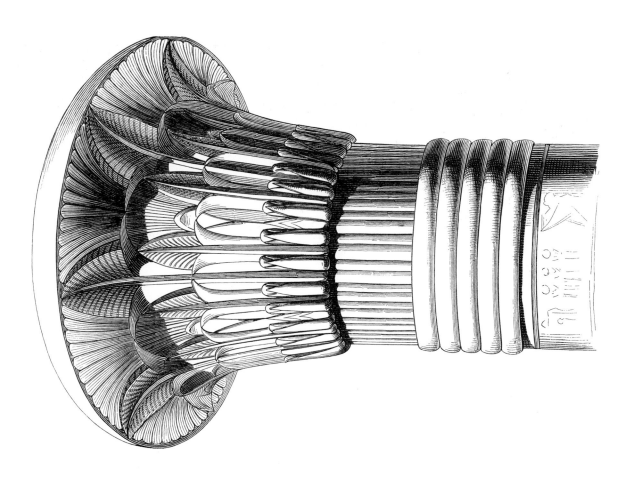

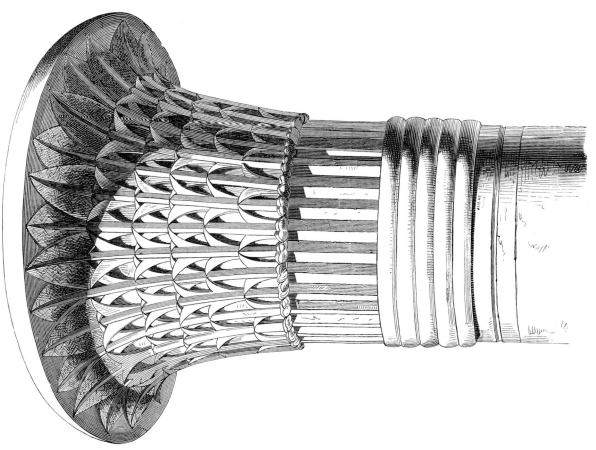

368

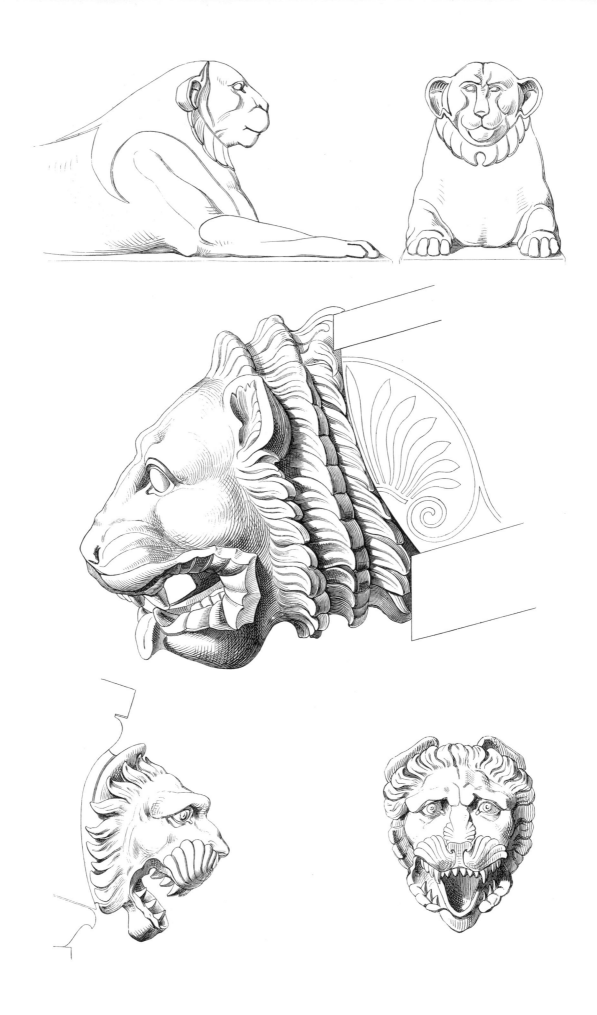

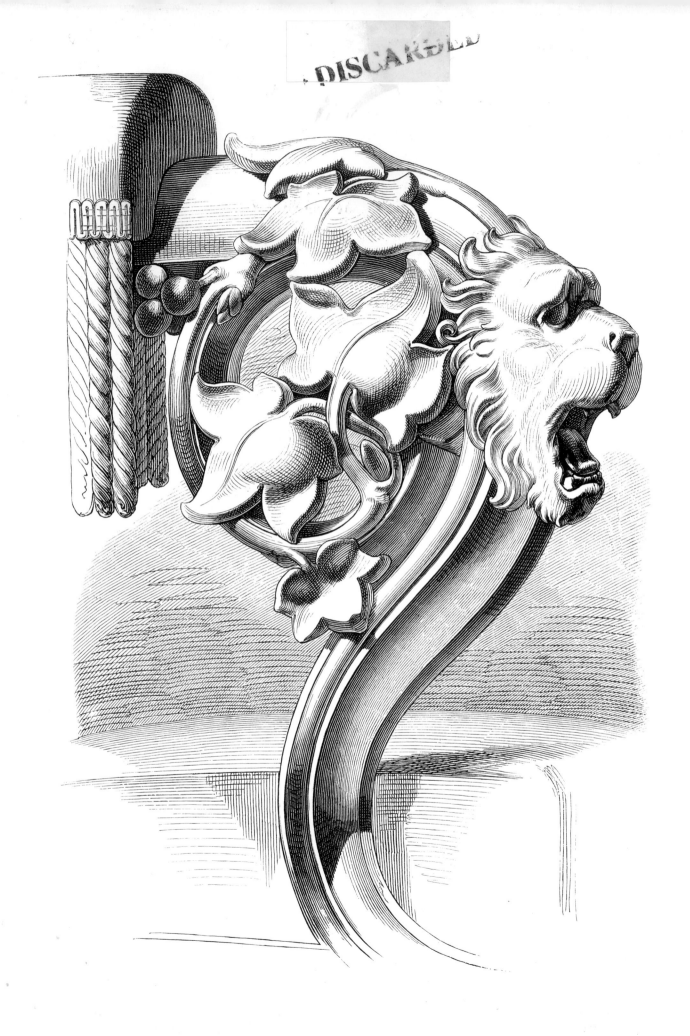

376